Title: Rich Decisions: A Year of Financial Planning and Wealth Building

What is a Rich Decision?

A rich decision typically refers to a decision-making process that involves comprehensive information, thoughtful analysis, and consideration of various factors, resulting in a well-informed and nuanced choice.

Chapter 1: January - Setting Financial Goals for the Year Ahead
In January, we set the stage for the year by discussing how to establish realistic and achievable financial goals. We explore the importance of budgeting, saving, and investing, and how to align your financial goals with your personal values.

Chapter 2: February - Investment Strategies for Long-Term Wealth
This chapter delves into the world of long-term investments, discussing the power of compound interest and the benefits of investing in stocks, bonds, and index funds. We also explore the potential of real estate as a long-term wealth-building strategy.

Chapter 3: March - Understanding Crypto: Opportunities and Risks
March is dedicated to understanding the world of cryptocurrencies. We examine the opportunities and risks associated with this rapidly evolving asset class, providing insights on how to approach crypto investments with caution and informed decision-making.

Chapter 4: April - Tax Planning and Wealth Preservation
As tax season approaches, we discuss effective tax planning strategies to minimize liabilities and maximize wealth preservation. This chapter also covers the benefits of retirement accounts, tax-efficient investing, and charitable giving.

Chapter 5: May - Diversification: Building a Resilient Investment Portfolio
In May, we focus on the importance of diversification in investment portfolios. We explore different asset classes, such as stocks, bonds, real estate, and alternative investments, and discuss how to construct a well-balanced and resilient portfolio.

Chapter 6: June - Navigating Market Volatility and Risk Management
This chapter addresses the challenges of market volatility and the principles of risk management. We provide insights on how to navigate turbulent markets, manage investment risks, and stay focused on long-term financial goals.

Chapter 7: July - Real Estate Investments: Opportunities and Pitfalls
July is dedicated to real estate investments. We explore the potential for wealth creation through real estate, including rental properties, real estate investment trusts (REITs), and real estate crowdfunding, while also highlighting potential pitfalls and risks.

Chapter 8: August - The Power of Passive Income and Dividend
Investing
In August, we discuss the concept of passive income and the benefits
of dividend investing. We explore strategies for building a
portfolio that generates regular income streams, providing financial
stability and long-term wealth growth.

Chapter 9: September - Retirement Planning and Long-Term Financial
Security
This chapter focuses on retirement planning, discussing the
importance of early and consistent retirement savings, as well as
the various retirement accounts and investment vehicles available to
build long-term financial security.

Chapter 10: October - Harnessing the Potential of Technology in
Investing
In October, we explore the latest financial tools and technologies
that are transforming the investment landscape. From robo-advisors
to algorithmic trading and fintech innovations, we discuss how
technology can enhance investment strategies.

Chapter 11: November - Sustainable and Ethical Investing for the
Future
This chapter delves into the growing trend of sustainable and
ethical investing. We discuss how investors can align their
financial goals with their values by supporting companies with
strong environmental, social, and governance (ESG) practices.

Chapter 12: December - Reflecting on the Year and Planning for the
Future
In December, we reflect on the year's financial decisions and
outcomes, and we lay the groundwork for the year ahead. We emphasize
the importance of continuous learning, adaptation, and long-term
financial planning as key components of wealth building.

Bonus, Chapter: Unlocking the Power of Music Investments

Introduction
Investing in the music industry offers a unique avenue for financial
growth and cultural influence. This chapter explores the potential
of music royalties and shares in an investor's portfolio, providing
a comprehensive guide on how to navigate this dynamic market.

Creating the Right Mindset: A Prelude to Rich Decisions: A Year of
Financial Wisdom

Before delving into the pages of Rich Decisions: A Year of Financial
Wisdom, let's take a moment to prepare ourselves mentally and
emotionally for the transformative journey that lies ahead. This
book is not just about financial strategies; it's a holistic guide
to wealth-building that encompasses mindset, personal development,
and intentional living. To fully absorb the insights and principles

shared within these pages, itâ€™s crucial to approach this journey
with a calm and focused mind.

Cultivating a Calm and Relaxing Mood

Imagine youâ€™re about to embark on a serene hike through a lush
forest. The air is crisp, the sunlight filters through the leaves,
and a gentle breeze whispers through the trees. As you open the
pages of this book, envision creating a mental space as tranquil as
that forest. Find a quiet corner, away from distractions, where you
can immerse yourself in the wisdom that awaits you.

Consider incorporating calming rituals into your reading experience.
Light a scented candle, play soft instrumental music, or brew a cup
of your favorite tea. These simple actions signal to your mind that
itâ€™s time to unwind, absorb, and reflect. As you create this
serene environment, youâ€™re setting the stage for a deeper
connection with the principles that will shape your financial
future.

The Power of Personal Development

Now, letâ€™s talk about personal development. As youâ€™re about to
embark on a journey of financial transformation, itâ€™s crucial to
recognize that true wealth extends beyond monetary value. Wealth
encompasses personal growth, fulfillment, and the positive impact
you make on yourself and others. Before diving into the specifics of
financial strategies, take a minute to reflect on your personal
development goals.

1.   Self-Reflection: Sit in a quiet space and reflect on your
        current stage of personal development. What are your
        strengths? What areas do you wish to improve? Be honest with
        yourself, as this self-awareness forms the foundation for
        meaningful growth.
2.   Goal Setting: Envision the person you aspire to become in
        the next year. What personal and professional goals align
        with your values and vision? Write down specific,
        measurable, and achievable goals that will contribute to
        your overall development.
3.   Learning Opportunities: Consider the skills and knowledge
        you need to enhance your personal and professional life. Are
        there courses, books, or workshops that align with your
        development goals? Create a list of learning opportunities
        to explore throughout the year.
4.   Mindfulness Practices: Incorporate mindfulness practices
        into your daily routine. Whether itâ€™s meditation, deep
        breathing exercises, or moments of quiet reflection, these
        practices can enhance your focus, reduce stress, and foster
        a positive mindset.

Preparing for Financial Success

With a calm and focused mindset, let’s shift our attention to your financial journey. As you read through “Rich **Decisions**,” keep in mind that financial success is not just about numbers on a balance sheet; it’s about aligning your financial decisions with your values and vision for a fulfilling life.

1. Values Assessment: Before diving into the financial strategies outlined in the book, take a moment to clarify your values. What truly matters to you? What are your long-term aspirations? Understanding your values will guide your financial decisions in a way that aligns with your authentic self.
2. Financial Goals: Set clear and achievable financial goals for the year ahead. Whether it’s saving for a specific purpose, investing for long-term growth, or paying down debt, having defined goals provides direction and motivation on your financial journey.
3. Budgeting Exercise: Review your current financial situation by creating a detailed budget. Understand your income, expenses, and discretionary spending. Identify areas where you can save or invest more effectively. A well-managed budget is a cornerstone of financial success.
4. Emergency Fund: Ensure that you have an emergency fund in place. Life is unpredictable, and having a financial safety net provides peace of mind. Aim to set aside at least three to six months’ worth of living expenses in a readily accessible account.

Creating Your Action Plan

Now that you’ve set the stage for a calm and focused reading experience and laid the groundwork for personal and financial development, it’s time to create your action plan. This plan will serve as a roadmap for implementing the principles outlined in Rich Decisions.

1. Weekly Action Steps: Break down your personal and financial goals into manageable weekly action steps. What small, consistent actions can you take to progress toward your objectives? Write down specific tasks to accomplish each week.
2. Accountability Partner: Consider sharing your goals and action plan with a trusted friend, family member, or mentor. Having an accountability partner can provide support, encouragement, and an external perspective on your journey.
3. Reflective Journaling: Keep a reflective journal throughout your reading journey. Document your insights, challenges, and victories. Regular journaling helps reinforce your commitment to personal and financial growth and allows you to track your progress.
4. Mindfulness Practices: Integrate mindfulness practices into your daily routine. Whether it’s a brief morning meditation, a mindful walk, or gratitude exercises, these

practices will enhance your ability to stay present, make intentional decisions, and cultivate a positive mindset.

Embracing the Journey

As you turn the pages of Rich Decisions: A Year of Financial Wisdom, remember that this is not just a book; itâ€™s an invitation to a transformative journey. Approach each chapter with an open heart and an inquisitive mind. Allow the wisdom shared within these pages to resonate with your unique goals, values, and aspirations.

In the moments of challenge, reflect on the calming environment youâ€™ve created and the personal development goals youâ€™ve set. In times of success, celebrate the alignment of your financial decisions with your vision for a rich and fulfilling life.

May your journey through Rich Decisions be not only a guide to financial wisdom but also a catalyst for personal and spiritual growth. Hereâ€™s to creating a life of abundance, purpose, and prosperity.

Onward to your rich decisions!

Chapter 1: January –

Setting Financial Goals for the Year Ahead
In January, we set the stage for the year by discussing how to establish realistic and achievable financial goals. We explore the importance of budgeting, saving, and investing, and how to align your financial goals with your personal values.

Crafting Financial Success: Establishing and Achieving Realistic Goals.

Establishing realistic and achievable financial goals is the compass guiding individuals towards financial success. This exploration delves into the intricacies of goal setting, emphasizing the crucial role of budgeting, saving, investing, and aligning financial aspirations with personal values. Understanding this holistic approach empowers individuals to navigate the journey towards financial well-being with clarity and purpose.

  Setting Realistic and Achievable Financial Goals

1. Define Clear Objectives:
Start by articulating specific, measurable, and time-bound financial goals.
Whether it's buying a home, saving for education, or retiring comfortably, clarity is the first step towards achievement.

2. Prioritize Goals:

Recognize the hierarchy of your financial   goals.
Prioritize them based on urgency, importance, and feasibility,
creating a roadmap for focused attainment.

3. Consider Short-Term and Long-Term:
 Balance short-term needs with long-term aspirations.
Allocate resources to address immediate financial concerns while
strategically planning for the future.

4. Account for Life Changes:
 Acknowledge that life is dynamic, and goals may evolve.
Regularly reassess and adjust financial objectives to align with
changing circumstances.

II. The Foundation: Budgeting.

1. Track Income and Expenses:
Create a comprehensive budget by tracking all sources of income and
categorizing expenditures.
Understanding where your money goes forms the basis of effective
financial management.

2. Differentiate Between Needs and Wants:
Distinguish between essential needs and discretionary spending.
Allocate resources according to priorities, ensuring necessities are
met before indulging in non-essential expenses.

3. Emergency Fund: A Financial Safety Net:
Establish an emergency fund to cover unexpected expenses.
Having a financial safety net prevents the need to dip into savings
or incur debt during challenging times.

4. Regularly Review and Adjust:
Periodically review your budget to ensure alignment with financial
goals and lifestyle changes.
Adjust spending patterns and savings contributions accordingly.

III. The Power of Saving.

1. Automate Savings:
Set up automatic transfers to savings accounts to ensure consistent
saving habits.
Automation fosters discipline and prevents the temptation to spend
funds earmarked for savings.

2. Cultivate a Savings Mindset:
Embrace saving as a non-negotiable aspect of financial planning.
Allocate a portion of income towards savings before addressing other
discretionary expenses.

3. Emergency Fund and Short-Term Goals:
 Allocate funds to an emergency fund and short-term savings goals.
Separate accounts for different objectives enhance financial
organization and clarity.

4. Harness the Power of Compounding:
 Invest in interest-bearing accounts or investment vehicles to
 capitalize on the compounding effect.
Even small, consistent contributions can lead to substantial growth
over time.

IV. Strategic Investing for Long-Term Growth.

1. Understand Risk Tolerance:
 Evaluate your risk tolerance to align investment strategies with
 your comfort level.
Balancing risk and return is crucial in constructing a diversified
and resilient investment portfolio.

2. Diversification Across Asset Classes:
 Diversify investments across stocks, bonds, and other asset classes
 to spread risk.
Asset allocation should align with your investment horizon and
financial goals.

3. Regular Portfolio Reviews:
 Periodically review and rebalance your investment portfolio.
Adjust allocations based on market conditions, changes in risk
tolerance, and evolving financial goals.

4. Explore Tax-Efficient Strategies:
 Consider tax-efficient investment strategies to minimize tax
 liabilities.
Utilize tax-advantaged accounts and engage with professionals for
tax-conscious investment planning.

V. Aligning Financial Goals with Personal Values.

1. Define Personal Values:
 Clarify your personal values and priorities in life.
Understanding what truly matters to you provides a foundation for
aligning financial goals with your intrinsic motivations.

2. Incorporate Values into Goals:
Integrate personal values into your financial goals.
This alignment enhances motivation and satisfaction in working
towards objectives that resonate with your beliefs.

3. Socially Responsible Investing:
Consider socially responsible or sustainable investing options that
align with your values.
Investing in companies that reflect your ethical standards
contributes to both financial and social goals.

4. Philanthropy and Giving Back:
Incorporate charitable giving into your financial plan if
philanthropy aligns with your values.

Contributing to causes that matter to you extends the impact of your
financial success to the broader community.

VI. Continuous Evaluation and Adaptation.

1.   Regular Financial Check-Ups:
Conduct regular financial check-ups to assess progress towards
goals.
This ongoing evaluation allows for timely adjustments and
adaptations based on changing circumstances, market conditions, and
personal priorities.

2.   Learning and Continuous Improvement:
 Stay informed about financial matters, investment strategies, and
 economic trends.
Continuous learning empowers you to make informed decisions, adapt
to changes, and optimize your financial plan.

3.   Professional Guidance:
Seek advice from financial professionals, including financial
advisors, accountants, and estate planners.
Professional guidance ensures that your financial strategies align
with your goals and adhere to best practices.

4.   Adapting to Life Changes:
Life is dynamic, and circumstances may change unexpectedly.
Be prepared to adapt your financial goals and strategies in response
to life events, such as marriage, having children, or changes in
employment.

VII. Achieving Financial Harmony.

In conclusion, achieving financial harmony is a multifaceted journey
that involves the meticulous establishment of realistic goals,
disciplined budgeting, strategic saving, and informed investing.
Aligning financial goals with personal values adds a layer of
purpose and fulfillment to the pursuit of financial success.

Remember that financial well-being is not a one-time accomplishment
but a continuous process of evaluation, adaptation, and growth. By
staying focused on your objectives, embracing a savings mindset, and
making deliberate choices that resonate with your values, you can
navigate the financial landscape with confidence and purpose.

In the tapestry of financial success, every decision, from setting
goals to making investment choices, contributes to the realization
of your aspirations. As you navigate this journey, remember that
financial success is not solely about accumulating wealth but about
attaining a state of financial well-being that aligns with your
unique values and life aspirations.

Chapter 2: February -

Investment Strategies for Long-Term Wealth
This chapter delves into the world of long-term investments, discussing the power of compound interest and the benefits of investing in stocks, bonds, and index funds. We also explore the potential of real estate as a long-term wealth-building strategy.

What's is Compound interest ?

Compound interest is a powerful financial concept where interest is calculated not only on the initial principal amount but also on the accumulated interest from previous periods. In other words, interest is earned not just on the initial investment but also on the interest that has been added to the principal over time.

Compound interest leads to exponential growth, meaning that the interest earned or charged keeps increasing as time goes on. This is in contrast to simple interest, where interest is calculated only on the original principal.

Compound interest plays a crucial role in financial planning and investing, as it allows investments to grow faster over time. It is a fundamental concept in areas like savings accounts, loans, mortgages, and investment vehicles like certificates of deposit (CDs) and bonds. Understanding compound interest is key to making informed financial decisions and maximizing the growth of your investments over the long term.

Unlocking Wealth: The Dynamics of Long-Term Investments.

In the journey towards financial prosperity, long-term investments stand as formidable pillars, guiding individuals on a path of wealth accumulation and financial security. This comprehensive exploration delves into the intricacies of long-term investments, emphasizing the transformative power of compound interest and the diverse benefits of allocating funds to stocks, bonds, index funds, and real estate. As we navigate this financial landscape, we'll unravel the dynamics that make long-term investments a cornerstone of wealth-building strategies.

I. The Foundation: Compound Interest

1. Understanding Compound Interest:
 At its core, compound interest is the mechanism that allows money to grow exponentially over time.
Unlike simple interest, compound interest incorporates the interest earned in previous periods into the principal amount, leading to accelerated growth.

2. The Power of Time:
Time is the most potent ally in the realm of compound interest. Starting early amplifies the impact of compounding, enabling individuals to harness the full potential of their investments.

3.   Compounding Frequency:
The frequency at which interest compounds plays a crucial role.
More frequent compounding, such as quarterly or monthly, enhances
the growth rate.

4.   Risk Mitigation and Volatility:
Long-term investments provide a buffer against short-term market
volatility.
The compounding effect smoothens the impact of market fluctuations,
fostering resilience in the face of economic uncertainties.

II. Investing in Stocks: The Engine of Growth

1.   Stocks as Ownership:
 Investing in stocks means becoming a partial owner of a company.
Stockholders share in the company's profits through dividends and
capital appreciation.

2.   Historical Stock Market Performance:
Despite short-term fluctuations, historical data demonstrates the
long-term growth potential of the stock market.
Stocks have consistently outpaced other asset classes over extended
periods.

3.   Diversification Strategies:
 Diversifying stock investments across industries and market sectors
 mitigates risk.
A well-balanced portfolio minimizes exposure to the vulnerabilities
of individual stocks.

4.   Dividend Investing:
Dividend-paying stocks contribute to a steady income stream for
investors.
Reinvesting dividends through a DRIP (Dividend Reinvestment Plan)
amplifies the compounding effect.

III. Bonds: Stability and Income

1.   Role of Bonds in a Portfolio:
  Bonds provide stability and income to an investment portfolio.
Their fixed-interest payments offer a predictable cash flow,
appealing to risk-averse investors.

2.   Government and Corporate Bonds:
Government bonds, such as Treasury bonds, are considered low-risk,
while corporate bonds offer higher yields with increased risk.
Investors tailor their bond allocations based on risk tolerance and
income objectives.

3.   Bond Maturity and Duration:
The maturity period and duration of bonds impact their risk and
return characteristics.
Long-term bonds may offer higher yields but come with increased
interest rate risk.

4. Balancing Risk and Reward:
Diversifying between stocks and bonds strikes a balance between
growth potential and risk mitigation.
Rebalancing the portfolio periodically ensures alignment with
investment goals.

IV. Index Funds: Harnessing Market Trends.

1. Passive Investing with Index Funds:
Index funds replicate the performance of a market index, providing
broad market exposure.
Passive investing, through index funds, offers a cost-effective and
low-maintenance approach.

2. Diversification and Cost Efficiency:
Index funds inherently offer diversification by tracking the
performance of entire markets or specific sectors.
Their low expense ratios make them attractive for cost-conscious
investors.

3. Avoiding Market Timing Pitfalls:
Timing the market consistently is a challenging endeavor.
 Index funds eliminate the need for market timing, allowing
 investors to participate in overall market growth.

4. Long-Term Consistency:
The buy-and-hold strategy with index funds aligns with long-term
investment goals.
Consistency and discipline are key to reaping the rewards of market
growth.

V. Real Estate: Building Wealth Brick by Brick.

1. Real Estate as a Tangible Asset:
 Investing in real estate provides tangible ownership of physical
 assets.
 Properties have the potential for appreciation, rental income, and
 tax benefits.

2. Rental Properties:
Owning rental properties generates a steady stream of income through
tenant rents.
 Real estate can act as a hedge against inflation, with property
 values often rising over time.

3. Real Estate Investment Trusts (REITs):
REITs offer a convenient way for investors to access the real estate
market without directly owning properties.
REITs pool funds from multiple investors to invest in a diversified
portfolio of income-generating real estate assets.

4. Real Estate Crowdfunding:

An emerging trend, real estate crowdfunding platforms enable
individuals to invest in specific real estate projects with
relatively lower capital.
Investors can diversify across various projects, reducing the risk
associated with a single property.

5. Potential Pitfalls and Risks:
While real estate can be a lucrative long-term investment, it comes
with its own set of challenges.
 Market fluctuations, property management issues, and economic
 downturns can impact real estate values and returns.

6. Tax Advantages:
 Real estate investments offer tax advantages, including deductions
 for mortgage interest, property depreciation, and operating
 expenses.
Understanding and leveraging these tax benefits enhances the overall
financial attractiveness of real estate.

VI. Strategies for Long-Term Success

1. Set Clear Investment Goals:
Define specific, measurable, and achievable long-term investment
goals.
Having a clear roadmap guides decision-making and helps stay focused
on the bigger picture.

2. Diversification and Asset Allocation:
Diversify investments across different asset classes to spread risk.
Regularly assess and rebalance the portfolio to maintain an optimal
asset allocation strategy.

3. Regular Contributions and Dollar-Cost Averaging:
Consistent contributions to investment accounts, regardless of
market conditions, capitalize on dollar-cost averaging.
This strategy mitigates the impact of short-term market volatility.

4. Emergency Fund and Liquidity:
  Maintain a sufficient emergency fund to cover unexpected expenses
  and prevent the need for premature liquidation of investments.
Liquidity ensures flexibility in navigating financial challenges.

5. Reinvest Dividends and Returns:
 Reinvesting dividends and returns compounds the growth potential of
 investments.
Automatic dividend reinvestment plans facilitate this process.

6. Monitor and Adjust:
Regularly monitor the performance of investments and adjust
strategies based on changing financial goals and market conditions.
Staying informed empowers investors to make well-informed decisions.

VII. Addressing Risks and Mitigation Strategies

1. Market Risks:
Acknowledge the inherent risks in the market, including economic
downturns, geopolitical events, and sector-specific challenges.
Diversification and a long-term perspective help weather short-term
market fluctuations.

2. Inflation Risk:
Inflation erodes the purchasing power of money over time.
Invest in assets with the potential for returns that outpace
inflation, such as equities and real estate.

3. Interest Rate Risk:
Fluctuations in interest rates impact the performance of bonds and
other interest-sensitive investments.
Understand the relationship between interest rates and investment
values.

4. Leverage and Debt Risk:
While leverage can amplify returns, it also increases the risk
associated with investments.
Use leverage judiciously, considering the potential impact on
investment stability.

5. Economic and Industry Risks:
Certain industries and sectors may face unique challenges due to
economic shifts or technological advancements.
Stay informed about industry trends and adapt the portfolio
accordingly.

VIII. The Psychological Aspect of Long-Term Investing

1. Patience and Discipline:
Long-term investing requires patience and discipline to withstand
short-term market volatility.
Avoid reactionary decisions based on emotional responses to market
fluctuations.

2. Behavioural Biases:
Recognize common behavioral biases, such as loss aversion and herd
mentality, that can influence investment decisions.
A mindful approach helps counteract these biases.

3. Embrace Market Volatility:
Rather than fearing market volatility, view it as an inherent part
of the investment journey.
Volatility creates opportunities for buying undervalued assets.

4. Adaptability to Changing Goals:
Life circumstances and financial goals evolve over time.
Maintain flexibility in adapting investment strategies to align with
changing objectives.

IX. The Role of Professional Guidance.

1. Financial Advisors:
 Engaging with a qualified financial advisor provides personalized
 insights and strategies tailored to individual goals.
A professional advisor helps navigate complex financial landscapes.

2. Continuous Learning:
Stay informed about changes in financial regulations, market trends,
and investment strategies.
Continuous learning empowers investors to make informed decisions.

3. Regular Portfolio Reviews:
Schedule regular portfolio reviews with financial professionals to
assess performance and adjust strategies.
Professional guidance adds a layer of expertise to the investment
process.

X. The Future of Long-Term Investments.

1. Technological Innovations:
Advancements in technology, including artificial intelligence and
blockchain, are influencing the landscape of long-term investments.
Explore innovative platforms and tools that enhance investment
efficiency.

2. Sustainable and ESG Investing:
The rise of sustainable and ESG (Environmental, Social, Governance)
investing reflects a shift towards socially responsible investment
choices.
Consider integrating sustainable principles into long-term
investment strategies.

3. Globalization and International Diversification:
Globalization offers opportunities for international
diversification, providing exposure to diverse markets and
economies.
Evaluate the potential benefits of diversifying across borders.

XI. Conclusion: The Odyssey of Wealth Accumulation.

In conclusion, the world of long-term investments unfolds as an
intricate tapestry, weaving together the threads of compound
interest, diverse asset classes, and strategic financial planning.
Investors embarking on this odyssey must navigate the complexities
with prudence, understanding the nuances of each investment avenue
and embracing the principles that withstand the test of time.

Whether one traverses the dynamic terrain of stocks, seeks stability
in bonds, harnesses the simplicity of index funds, or ventures into
the realm of real estate, the common thread is the steadfast
commitment to long-term objectives. The transformative power of
compound interest acts as the North Star, guiding investors towards
the realization of financial goals and the accumulation of wealth
over time.

As the investment landscape evolves and new opportunities emerge, the fundamental principles of discipline, diversification, and adaptability remain the pillars of long-term success. By addressing risks, acknowledging the psychological aspects of investing, and leveraging professional guidance, individuals can navigate this odyssey with resilience and confidence. Ultimately, the journey towards financial prosperity is not a sprint but a marathonâ€"a carefully paced expedition that unfolds over years and decades, transforming aspirations into tangible wealth and enduring financial security.

Chapter 3: March -

Understanding Crypto: Cryptocurrencies are digital or virtual currencies that use cryptography for security and operate on decentralized networks based on blockchain technology. Unlike traditional currencies issued by governments and central banks, cryptocurrencies operate on a peer-to-peer network, allowing for secure and transparent transactions without the need for intermediaries.

Key features of cryptocurrencies include:

1. Decentralization: Cryptocurrencies operate on a decentralized network of computers (nodes), eliminating the need for a central authority like a bank or government. This decentralization contributes to transparency and reduces the risk of manipulation.

2. Blockchain Technology: Most cryptocurrencies utilize blockchain, a distributed ledger that records all transactions across a network. Blockchain ensures transparency, security, and immutability of transaction history.

3. Cryptography: Cryptocurrencies rely on cryptographic techniques to secure transactions and control the creation of new units. This cryptographic security makes it challenging for unauthorized parties to alter transaction data.

4. Limited Supply: Many cryptocurrencies have a capped supply, meaning there is a maximum limit on the number of units that can ever exist. For example, Bitcoin has a cap of 21 million coins, promoting scarcity and potentially influencing value over time.

5. Anonymity and Pseudonymity While transactions are recorded on the blockchain, the identities of users are often pseudonymous. Users are represented by cryptographic addresses rather than personal information. However, the level of anonymity varies between different cryptocurrencies.

6. Global Accessibility: Cryptocurrencies can be sent or received anywhere in the world, and transactions typically have lower

fees compared to traditional financial systems. This global
accessibility makes cryptocurrencies attractive for cross-border
transactions.

Bitcoin, created in 2009 by an unknown person or group using the
pseudonym Satoshi Nakamoto, was the first cryptocurrency and remains
the most well-known. Since then, thousands of alternative
cryptocurrencies (commonly referred to as altcoins) have been
developed, each with its unique features and use cases. Ethereum,
Ripple (XRP), Litecoin, and Cardano are examples of other prominent
cryptocurrencies. Cryptocurrencies can be used for various purposes,
including online transactions, investment, smart contracts, and as a
store of value.

Opportunities and Risks
March is dedicated to understanding the world of cryptocurrencies.
We examine the opportunities and risks associated with this rapidly
evolving asset class, providing insights on how to approach crypto
investments with caution and informed decision-making.

Navigating the World of Cryptocurrencies: Opportunities, Risks, and
Informed Decision-Making.

The realm of cryptocurrencies, marked by its decentralized nature
and groundbreaking blockchain technology, has become a captivating
frontier in the financial landscape. In this exploration, we unravel
the complexities of cryptocurrencies, shedding light on the
opportunities and risks that accompany this rapidly evolving asset
class. Understanding how to approach crypto investments with caution
and informed decision-making is crucial in navigating the dynamic
and sometimes volatile world of digital currencies.

I. Understanding Cryptocurrencies.

1. Decentralization and Blockchain:
Cryptocurrencies operate on decentralized networks, eliminating the
need for intermediaries like banks.
Blockchain, the underlying technology, ensures transparent and
secure transactions through a distributed ledger.

2. Bitcoin as the Pioneer:
Bitcoin, introduced in 2009, is the first and most well-known
cryptocurrency.
It laid the foundation for a multitude of alternative
cryptocurrencies, commonly referred to as altcoins.

3. Diverse Cryptocurrency Ecosystem:
The cryptocurrency landscape encompasses a myriad of digital assets
with various use cases, including currencies, smart contracts, and
decentralized finance (DeFi) platforms.
Each cryptocurrency serves a specific purpose within its ecosystem.

4. Market Volatility:

Cryptocurrency prices are notoriously volatile, influenced by factors such as market sentiment, regulatory developments, and technological advancements.
The potential for rapid price fluctuations is a defining characteristic of the crypto market.

II. Opportunities in Cryptocurrency Investments.

1. Potential for High Returns:
The cryptocurrency market has witnessed substantial gains over short periods, leading to significant returns for some investors.
Early adopters of major cryptocurrencies, particularly Bitcoin, have experienced remarkable appreciation.

2. Innovation in Blockchain Technology:
Blockchain technology, the backbone of cryptocurrencies, has transformative potential across various industries.
Investing in cryptocurrencies allows participation in the development and adoption of innovative blockchain applications.

3. Diversification of Investment Portfolios:
Cryptocurrencies offer a means to diversify traditional investment portfolios.
Including digital assets can potentially enhance overall portfolio performance, especially in the context of uncorrelated asset classes.

4. Decentralized Finance (DeFi):
DeFi platforms leverage blockchain technology to provide decentralized alternatives to traditional financial services.
Investors can participate in lending, borrowing, and yield farming, potentially earning attractive returns.

III. Risks Associated with Cryptocurrency Investments.

1. Market Volatility and Speculative Nature:
Cryptocurrencies are highly speculative, and their prices can experience extreme volatility.
Investors should be prepared for rapid and unpredictable market movements.

2. Regulatory Uncertainty:
Regulatory frameworks for cryptocurrencies vary widely across countries and are subject to ongoing developments.
Changes in regulations can impact the legality and market acceptance of cryptocurrencies.

3. Security Concerns and Hacks:
The decentralized nature of cryptocurrencies doesn't make them immune to security risks.
Hacks, fraud, and vulnerabilities in exchanges or wallets can result in the loss of funds.

4. Lack of Consumer Protections:

Unlike traditional financial systems, cryptocurrencies often lack
the consumer protections provided by banks and financial
institutions.
Investors bear a higher level of responsibility for the security of
their assets.

IV. Approach to Crypto Investments with Caution

1. Thorough Research and Education:
 Before investing, thoroughly research the specific cryptocurrency,
 its use case, and the underlying technology.
Understanding the fundamentals is crucial for making informed
investment decisions.

2. Diversification and Risk Management:
Diversify cryptocurrency investments to mitigate the impact of
volatility on the overall portfolio.
Allocate only a portion of the investment portfolio to
cryptocurrencies, aligning with risk tolerance.

3. Secure Storage and Custody:
Use reputable wallets and exchanges that prioritize security
measures.
Consider hardware wallets for offline storage to reduce exposure to
online threats.

4. Stay Informed about Regulatory Changes:
Monitor regulatory developments in the countries where you operate.
Adapt investment strategies based on evolving regulatory landscapes.

5. Long-Term Perspective:
Approach cryptocurrency investments with a long-term perspective
rather than succumbing to short-term market fluctuations.
Avoid making impulsive decisions based on emotional reactions to
price movements.

V. Conclusion: Navigating the Crypto Seas with Prudence

In conclusion, navigating the world of cryptocurrencies demands a
delicate balance between recognizing the opportunities they present
and acknowledging the associated risks. While digital assets offer
potential for high returns and innovation in blockchain technology,
the market's inherent volatility and regulatory uncertainties
require investors to exercise caution and diligence.

Approaching crypto investments with informed decision-making
involves continuous learning, risk management strategies, and a
commitment to security. As the cryptocurrency landscape evolves,
staying abreast of technological advancements, regulatory changes,
and market dynamics becomes paramount for those seeking to
participate in this rapidly evolving asset class.

Cryptocurrencies represent a paradigm shift in the financial world,
offering new possibilities and challenges. By treading carefully,

staying informed, and adopting a prudent investment approach,
individuals can navigate the crypto seas with resilience and
position themselves for potential benefits while mitigating the
inherent risks.

Chapter 4: April –

Tax Planning and Wealth Preservation
As tax season approaches, we discuss effective tax planning
strategies to minimize liabilities and maximize wealth preservation.
This chapter also covers the benefits of retirement accounts, tax-
efficient investing, and charitable giving.

Crafting a Financial Fortress: Effective Tax Planning Strategies for
Wealth Preservation

Effective tax planning stands as a cornerstone in the architecture
of financial well-being, offering a strategic framework to minimize
tax liabilities and optimize wealth preservation. This comprehensive
exploration delves into the intricacies of tax planning, unraveling
the benefits of retirement accounts, tax-efficient investing, and
the philanthropic avenue of charitable giving. Understanding these
strategies empowers individuals to navigate the complex landscape of
taxation, ensuring the preservation and growth of their wealth.

I. Foundations of Effective Tax Planning

1. Strategic Income Deferral:

Delaying the receipt of income, when feasible, can reduce current
tax liabilities.
Strategies include deferring bonuses, capital gains realization, and
income from retirement accounts.

2. Optimizing Deductions:

Leveraging available deductions, such as mortgage interest, medical
expenses, and charitable contributions, contributes to reducing
taxable income.
Itemizing deductions or utilizing tax credits enhances overall tax
efficiency.

3. Tax-Efficient Asset Allocation:

Strategically allocating assets across taxable and tax-advantaged
accounts optimizes the tax treatment of investment gains and income.
Consideration of tax implications guides portfolio construction.

4. Roth Conversions and Backdoor Roth IRAs:

Converting traditional retirement account funds to Roth IRAs can
create tax-free income in retirement.

High-income earners may utilize backdoor Roth contributions for tax-efficient retirement savings.

II. Maximizing Retirement Account Benefits

1. Contributions to Employer-Sponsored Plans:

Maximizing contributions to employer-sponsored retirement plans, such as 401(k)s, reduces current taxable income.
Employer matches provide additional opportunities for wealth accumulation.

2. Individual Retirement Accounts (IRAs):
Contributing to traditional IRAs offers immediate tax benefits, while Roth IRAs provide tax-free withdrawals in retirement.
Understanding income limits and contribution rules optimizes IRA strategies.

3. Health Savings Accounts (HSAs):

Contributions to HSAs, when used for qualified medical expenses, are tax-deductible.
HSAs also serve as a unique long-term savings vehicle, allowing for tax-free growth.

4. Required Minimum Distributions (RMDs):

Managing RMDs from retirement accounts is crucial to avoid unnecessary tax burdens.
Strategies include strategic distribution planning and considering qualified charitable distributions.

III. Tax-Efficient Investing Strategies

1. Harvesting Capital Losses:

Strategically realizing capital losses offsets gains, minimizing tax liabilities.
Tax loss harvesting can be employed to rebalance portfolios without adverse tax consequences.

2. Utilizing Tax-Efficient Funds:

Investing in tax-efficient funds, such as index funds or ETFs, reduces taxable distributions.
Minimizing turnover and avoiding high-dividend funds contribute to tax efficiency.

3. Asset Location Strategies:

Placing tax-inefficient assets in tax-advantaged accounts and tax-efficient assets in taxable accounts optimizes overall tax treatment.
This approach maximizes after-tax returns.

4. Gifting and Inheritance Planning:

Leveraging the annual gift tax exclusion allows for tax-efficient
wealth transfer.
Strategic estate planning, including step-up in basis
considerations, minimizes tax implications for heirs.

IV. Charitable Giving for Tax Efficiency

1. Donor-Advised Funds (DAFs):

Contributions to DAFs provide an immediate tax deduction, allowing
for flexible charitable giving over time.
Strategic planning with DAFs aligns charitable goals with tax
efficiency.

2. Qualified Charitable Distributions (QCDs):

Directly transferring funds from IRAs to charities through QCDs
satisfies RMDs and minimizes taxable income.
QCDs are especially advantageous for retirees with charitable
inclinations.

3. Appreciated Securities Donations:

Donating appreciated securities to charities avoids capital gains
taxes.
This strategy aligns philanthropy with tax efficiency, maximizing
the impact of charitable contributions.

4. Legacy and Estate Charitable Planning:

Incorporating charitable elements into estate plans, such as
charitable remainder trusts (CRTs) or charitable lead trusts (CLTs),
combines philanthropy with tax benefits.
These structures offer potential income tax deductions and estate
tax benefits.

V. Professional Guidance and Continuous Adaptation

1. Collaboration with Tax Professionals:

Engaging with tax professionals, including CPAs and financial
advisors, ensures comprehensive tax planning aligned with individual
circumstances.
Regular consultations enable adjustments based on changing tax laws
and personal financial situations.

2. Continuous Adaptation to Tax Laws:

Tax laws undergo changes, necessitating a proactive approach to
adaptation.

Remaining informed about legislative updates and incorporating them into tax strategies is vital for long-term effectiveness.

3. Regular Financial Check-Ups:

Conducting regular financial check-ups allows for reassessment of tax strategies based on evolving financial goals and external factors.
Adjustments to tax planning are integral to maintaining optimal wealth preservation strategies.

VI. Conclusion: A Strategic Tapestry for Wealth Preservation

In conclusion, effective tax planning unfolds as a strategic tapestry, intricately weaving together various threads to minimize tax liabilities and preserve wealth. By embracing opportunities presented by retirement accounts, tax-efficient investing, and charitable giving, individuals craft a robust financial fortress that withstands the tests of time and taxation.

The benefits of strategic income deferral, optimizing deductions, and maximizing the advantages of retirement accounts contribute to a tax-efficient framework. Incorporating tax-efficient investing strategies and navigating the landscape of charitable giving further fortify this structure, aligning financial goals with philanthropic endeavors.

As the financial landscape evolves and tax laws undergo changes, the commitment to continuous adaptation and collaboration with tax professionals becomes paramount. Through regular financial check-ups and a proactive approach to tax planning, individuals navigate the dynamic terrain of taxation with resilience and precision, ensuring that their wealth preservation strategies remain effective and aligned with their overarching financial objectives.

Now let's take a Look into positive self talk and what it is.

Positive self-talk is the intentional practice of maintaining a constructive and optimistic inner dialogue with oneself. It involves consciously choosing affirming and encouraging statements to counteract negative thoughts and self-doubt. This practice aims to promote a healthier mindset, boost self-esteem, and enhance overall well-being. Instead of dwelling on limitations or setbacks, individuals engaging in positive self-talk focus on their strengths, accomplishments, and potential for growth. The goal is to cultivate a positive and empowering narrative within the mind, fostering resilience, motivation, and a more optimistic outlook on life. Positive self-talk is a tool used in various contexts, such as personal development, stress management, and building mental resilience.

Here are 12 things you can do to master your positive self talk in a few days.

1.   Practice self-awareness: Identify negative thoughts as they arise.
2.   Challenge negative beliefs: Question and reframe pessimistic thinking.
3.   Cultivate self-compassion: Treat yourself with kindness and understanding.
4.   Set realistic goals: Break them down into achievable steps.
5.   Surround yourself with positivity: Engage with uplifting people and content.
6.   Create affirmations: Develop positive statements to counteract negativity.
7.   Focus on strengths: Acknowledge and leverage your personal strengths.
8.   Practice gratitude: Reflect on the positive aspects of your life regularly.
9.   Mindful breathing: Use deep breaths to center yourself and manage stress.
10.   Visualization techniques: Picture success and positive outcomes.
11.   Learn from setbacks: View challenges as opportunities for growth.
12.   Seek professional support: Consider therapy or coaching for guidance.

Hereâ€™s a bonus 12 more tips on positive self talk.

1.   Positive self-talk involves consciously cultivating optimistic and constructive inner dialogue.
2.   Itâ€™s a practice where individuals replace negative thoughts with affirming and empowering statements.
3.   This approach focuses on promoting self-encouragement, resilience, and a healthier mindset.
4.   By embracing positive self-talk, individuals can enhance their overall mental and emotional well-being.
5.   Benefits include reduced stress levels, as constructive thoughts can mitigate the impact of challenges.
6.   Positive self-talk fosters a more optimistic outlook, promoting a sense of hope and motivation.
7.   Improved self-esteem is a notable outcome, as affirmations build a positive self-image.
8.   This practice aids in developing a growth mindset, encouraging learning and adaptability.
9.   Enhanced problem-solving skills often result from maintaining a positive and solution-oriented mindset.
10.   Positive self-talk contributes to better relationships, as a positive mindset can positively influence interactions with others.
11.   Increased resilience is a key advantage, helping individuals bounce back from setbacks more effectively.
12.   Overall, embracing positive self-talk is a valuable tool for personal development and creating a more fulfilling life.

Chapter 5: May -

 Diversification: Building a Resilient Investment Portfolio
In May, we focus on the importance of diversification in investment
portfolios. We explore different asset classes, such as stocks,
bonds, real estate, and alternative investments, and discuss how to
construct a well-balanced and resilient portfolio.

Constructing Fortitude: The Crucial Role of Diversification in
Investment Portfolios

Diversification stands as the bedrock of prudent investment
strategy, offering a shield against the uncertainties of financial
markets. This exploration delves into the paramount importance of
diversification in investment portfolios, unraveling the dynamics of
various asset classes, including stocks, bonds, real estate, and
alternative investments. Understanding how to construct a well-
balanced and resilient portfolio becomes instrumental in navigating
the complexities of the investment landscape and mitigating risks
associated with market fluctuations.

I. The Essence of Diversification

1. Risk Mitigation:
Diversification is a risk management strategy that involves
spreading investments across different assets to minimize exposure
to the poor performance of a single investment.
The proverb "Don't put all your eggs in one basket" encapsulates the
essence of diversification.

2. Enhanced Portfolio Stability:
Diversified portfolios are less susceptible to extreme volatility,
providing a more stable and consistent investment experience.
This stability is particularly crucial during turbulent market
conditions.

3. Optimizing Risk-Return Tradeoff:
By combining assets with varying risk profiles, investors aim to
optimize the risk-return tradeoff.
Balancing risk and potential returns fosters a more resilient
portfolio.

4. Adaptability to Market Changes:
Diversification allows portfolios to adapt to changing market
dynamics, ensuring they are not overly exposed to specific sectors
or asset classes.
This adaptability is essential in navigating evolving economic
conditions.

II. Asset Classes: Building Blocks of Diversification

1. Stocks: The Engine of Growth:

Stocks represent ownership in companies and offer the potential for
capital appreciation.
 High-risk, high-reward, they form the growth-oriented component of
 diversified portfolios.

2. Bonds: Stability and Income:
Bonds are debt instruments that provide stability and regular
interest payments.
Considered safer than stocks, bonds contribute income and act as a
counterbalance to equity volatility.

3. Real Estate: Tangible Wealth Creation:
Investing in real estate involves ownership of physical properties,
providing potential for appreciation and rental income.
Real estate adds a tangible and often less correlated element to a
portfolio.

4. Alternative Investments: Beyond Tradition:
Alternative investments, including hedge funds, private equity, and
commodities, offer diversification beyond traditional asset classes.
They may have lower correlation with stocks and bonds, providing
unique risk-return profiles.

III. Constructing a Resilient Portfolio

1. Risk Tolerance Assessment:
Understanding individual risk tolerance is the foundation of
portfolio construction.
Investors with a higher risk tolerance may have a more substantial
allocation to stocks, while those with lower risk tolerance may lean
towards bonds.

2. Strategic Asset Allocation:
Determining the desired long-term mix of asset classes based on
financial goals and risk tolerance is the essence of strategic asset
allocation.
This establishes the broad framework for the portfolio.

3. Tactical Asset Allocation:
Tactical asset allocation involves adjusting the portfolio's
weightings based on short-term market conditions.
This dynamic approach allows investors to capitalize on perceived
opportunities or mitigate specific risks.

4. Rebalancing:
Regularly rebalancing the portfolio ensures that the asset
allocation aligns with the original strategic plan.
This involves selling assets that have performed well and
reallocating funds to underperforming or undervalued assets.

5. Global Diversification:
Investors should consider diversification not only across asset
classes but also geographically.

Global diversification reduces exposure to regional economic risks
and enhances opportunities for growth.

IV. The Importance of Correlation

1. Correlation: A Key Metric:
Understanding the correlation between different asset classes is
crucial in constructing a diversified portfolio.
Low or negative correlation implies that the assets do not move in
tandem, providing effective risk reduction.

2. Diversification Beyond Traditional Assets:
Including alternative investments that have low correlation with
traditional assets further enhances portfolio diversification.
This approach aims to minimize the impact of market-wide downturns.

V. Continuous Monitoring and Adaptation

1. Market Dynamics and Economic Trends:
Remaining vigilant to market dynamics, economic trends, and
geopolitical events allows for informed decision-making.
Adapting the portfolio to changing conditions is a key component of
effective diversification.

Chapter 6: June -

Navigating Market Volatility and Risk Management
This chapter addresses the challenges of market volatility and the
principles of risk management. We provide insights on how to
navigate turbulent markets, manage investment risks, and stay
focused on long-term financial goals.

Navigating market volatility and implementing effective risk
management strategies is crucial for investors seeking stability and
growth in their portfolios. In this comprehensive exploration, we'll
delve into the challenges posed by market volatility, the principles
of risk management, and insights on navigating turbulent markets
while staying focused on long-term financial goals.

Understanding Market Volatility.

Definition of Market Volatility:
Market volatility refers to the degree of variation in trading
prices over time. It is a key indicator of market uncertainty and
can result from various factors, including economic data,
geopolitical events, and changes in investor sentiment.

Challenges of Market Volatility:
1. Emotional Impact:Sharp market movements can evoke emotional
    responses, leading to impulsive decision-making.

2. Uncertainty:*Volatility introduces uncertainty, making it
    challenging to predict market movements accurately.
3. Increased Risk: Higher volatility often accompanies increased
    risk, impacting investment performance.

Principles of Risk Management

Risk Management Defined:
Risk management involves identifying, assessing, and mitigating
potential risks to protect investments and achieve long-term
financial objectives.

Key Principles:
1. Diversification: Spread investments across different asset
    classes to reduce the impact of a poor-performing investment on
    the overall portfolio.
2. Asset Allocation: Allocate assets strategically based on
    individual risk tolerance, financial goals, and market
    conditions.
3. Risk Tolerance Assessment: Evaluate your risk tolerance to
    ensure your investment strategy aligns with your comfort level.
4. Stop-Loss Orders: Implement stop-loss orders to automatically
    sell an asset when it reaches a predetermined price, limiting
    potential losses.
5. Continuous Monitoring: Regularly review and adjust your
    investment strategy based on changes in market conditions and
    personal financial goals.

Navigating Turbulent Markets

Strategies for Navigating Volatility:
1. Stay Informed: Keep abreast of market news and economic
    indicators to anticipate potential volatility triggers.
2. Long-Term Perspective: Focus on long-term financial goals rather
    than short-term market fluctuations.
3. Quality Investments: Invest in fundamentally sound companies
    with strong financials and growth potential.
4. Avoid Market Timing: Attempting to time the market is
    challenging; instead, adopt a disciplined, systematic investment
    approach.
5. Professional Guidance: Consider seeking advice from financial
    professionals to navigate complex market conditions.

Managing Investment Risks

Identifying and Mitigating Risks:
1. Risk Identification: Identify various types of risks, including
    market risk, credit risk, and liquidity risk.
2. Research and Due Diligence: Conduct thorough research before
    making investment decisions to mitigate unforeseen risks.
3. Stay Liquid: Maintain a level of liquidity to respond to
    unexpected financial needs or capitalize on investment
    opportunities.

4. Insurance Strategies: Explore insurance options to protect
    against specific risks, such as market downturns or health-
    related expenses.

Staying Focused on Long-Term Financial Goals

Importance of Long-Term Focus:
1. Market Fluctuations are Normal:
Understand that market fluctuations are part of the investment
journey and don't necessarily derail long-term plans.
2. Regular Portfolio Reviews: Periodically review and rebalance
    your portfolio to ensure alignment with evolving financial
    goals.
3. Emergency Fund: Maintain an emergency fund to cover unexpected
    expenses, reducing the need to liquidate investments during
    market downturns.
4. Goal Reassessment: Periodically reassess your financial goals,
    adjusting your investment strategy accordingly.

 Conclusion

In conclusion, successfully navigating market volatility requires a
combination of understanding its challenges, implementing robust
risk management principles, and adopting strategies that focus on
long-term financial goals. By staying informed, managing risks
effectively, and maintaining a disciplined investment approach,
investors can position themselves to weather turbulent markets and
achieve sustainable financial success. Remember, the journey toward
financial stability is a marathon, not a sprint.

Chapter 7: July -

 Real Estate Investments: Opportunities and Pitfalls
July is dedicated to real estate investments. We explore the
potential for wealth creation through real estate, including rental
properties, real estate investment trusts (REITs), and real estate
crowdfunding, while also highlighting potential pitfalls and risks.

Exploring Real Estate Investments for Wealth Creation: A
Comprehensive Analysis

Real estate investment is a dynamic and multifaceted avenue for
wealth creation, encompassing various strategies such as rental
properties, Real Estate Investment Trusts (REITs), and real estate
crowdfunding. This comprehensive exploration will delve into the
potential benefits of real estate investments, the diverse methods
available, and the associated risks and pitfalls.

Whats Are (REITs?

Real Estate Investment Trusts (REITs) are investment vehicles that
own, operate, or finance income-generating real estate across
various sectors. These trusts allow individuals to invest in large-

scale, income-producing real estate without having to directly manage or own the properties. REITs offer a way for investors to access diversified real estate portfolios, typically providing regular income in the form of dividends.

Key features of REITs include:

1.   Income Generation: The primary purpose of REITs is to generate income through the ownership and management of income-producing real estate properties. They often distribute the majority of their income to shareholders in the form of dividends.
2.   Diversification: REITs invest in a diverse range of real estate assets, which may include residential and commercial properties, hotels, shopping centers, office buildings, and more. This diversification helps spread risk across different types of real estate.
3.   Liquidity: REITs are traded on major stock exchanges, providing investors with liquidity compared to direct real estate investments, which can be less liquid.
4.   Transparency: REITs are subject to regulations that require transparency and reporting standards, providing investors with information about the performance and composition of the real estate portfolio.
5.   Tax Advantages: To qualify as a REIT, a company must distribute at least 90% of its taxable income to shareholders in the form of dividends. This structure allows REITs to avoid paying corporate income taxes at the entity level.
6.   Accessibility: REITs provide individual investors the opportunity to participate in real estate markets with relatively small amounts of capital. Investors can buy shares of publicly traded REITs through brokerage accounts.

There are two main types of REITs:

1.   Equity REITs: These primarily own and operate income-producing real estate. Income generated from rents and property sales is distributed to shareholders as dividends.
2.   Mortgage REITs (mREITs): These invest in real estate mortgages or mortgage-backed securities, generating income through interest on the loans. Income is distributed to shareholders as dividends.

Investing in REITs can offer diversification and income potential, but like any investment, they come with risks. The value of REIT shares can fluctuate based on factors such as interest rates, economic conditions, and the performance of the underlying real estate assets. Individuals considering REIT investments should carefully evaluate their financial goals and risk tolerance before investing.

Understanding Real Estate as an Investment

Definition and Importance:
Real estate investment involves acquiring, owning, and managing properties with the expectation of generating returns. It is a tangible asset class that has historically provided both income and appreciation, making it a crucial component of diversified investment portfolios.

Benefits of Real Estate Investment:

1.   Income Generation: Rental properties can generate regular income through tenant payments.
2.   Appreciation: Real estate has the potential to appreciate over time, providing capital gains.
3.   Diversification: Real estate offers diversification benefits, as it often behaves differently than traditional financial assets like stocks and bonds.
4.   Tax Advantages: Investors may benefit from tax advantages such as depreciation deductions and capital gains tax treatment.

Rental Properties: A Hands-On Approach

Advantages of Rental Properties:

1.   Steady Income: Rental properties can provide a consistent stream of rental income.
2.   Control and Decision-Making: Investors have direct control over property management decisions.
3.   Appreciation Potential: Properties may appreciate over time, increasing the asset's overall value.

Challenges and Risks:

1.   Property Management: Managing tenants, maintenance, and property-related issues can be time-consuming.
2.   Market Sensitivity: Real estate values are subject to market fluctuations.
3.   Liquidity Concerns: Selling a property can take time, and liquidity may be limited.

Real Estate Investment Trusts (REITs): A Passive Approach

What are REITs:
REITs are companies that own, operate, or finance income-generating real estate across various sectors, from residential to commercial properties. Investors can buy shares in a REIT, gaining exposure to real estate without direct ownership.

Advantages of REITs:

1.   Diversification: REITs offer diversification across a broad spectrum of real estate assets.

2.   Liquidity: REIT shares can be bought or sold on the stock exchange, providing liquidity.
3.   Professional Management: REITs are managed by professionals, reducing the need for hands-on involvement.

Challenges and Risks:

1.   Market Dependency: REITs can be influenced by overall market conditions and interest rate fluctuations.
2.   Dividend Sensitivity: Dividend payments, a key attraction for investors, can be impacted by economic downturns.
3.   Lack of Control: Investors have no direct control over the management decisions of the underlying real estate.

Real Estate Crowdfunding: A Modern Investment Avenue

What is Crowdfunding in Real Estate:
Real estate crowdfunding involves multiple investors contributing funds to finance a real estate project. This method allows investors to participate in larger deals with smaller capital contributions.

Advantages of Real Estate Crowdfunding:

1.   Access to Diverse Projects: Investors can choose from a variety of real estate projects across different locations and asset types.
2.   Lower Capital Requirement: Real estate crowdfunding allows investors to participate with relatively small amounts of capital.
3.   Professional Oversight: Crowdfunding platforms often provide professional management and oversight.

Challenges and Risks:

1.   Project Risks: Individual projects may not always succeed, leading to potential losses.
2.   Limited Control: Investors have limited control over project management decisions.
3.   Platform Risks: The success and security of real estate crowdfunding depend on the reliability of the chosen platform.

Potential Pitfalls and Risks in Real Estate Investments

1.   Market Fluctuations: Real estate values can be sensitive to economic conditions and market trends.
2.   Financing Risks: High levels of debt or unfavorable financing terms can amplify risks.
3.   Regulatory Changes: Changes in local or national regulations can impact the real estate market.
4.   Maintenance Costs: Unexpected maintenance or repair costs can erode returns.
5.   Tenant Issues: Vacancies, difficult tenants, or non-payment can pose challenges for rental property owners.

Strategies for Mitigating Risks

1.   Thorough Due Diligence: Conduct extensive research on potential properties, markets, or crowdfunding platforms.
2.   Diversification: Spread investments across different types of real estate and geographic locations.
3.   Professional Advice: Seek advice from real estate professionals, financial advisors, and legal experts.
4.   Emergency Reserves: Maintain sufficient reserves to cover unexpected expenses or periods of low income.
5.   Stay Informed: Keep abreast of market trends, economic indicators, and regulatory changes.

Conclusion

In conclusion, real estate investment presents diverse opportunities for wealth creation, from the hands-on approach of managing rental properties to the passive nature of investing in REITs and the modern avenue of real estate crowdfunding. While the potential benefits are substantial, itâ€™s crucial to acknowledge and address the associated risks and pitfalls. Adopting a well-informed and strategic approach, along with ongoing risk management, can empower investors to navigate the complexities of real estate investment and unlock its full wealth-building potential.

Chapter 8: August -

 The Power of Passive Income and Dividend Investing
In August, we discuss the concept of passive income and the benefits of dividend investing. We explore strategies for building a portfolio that generates regular income streams, providing financial stability and long-term wealth growth.

Exploring Passive Income and Dividend Investing for Long-Term Wealth Building

Passive income, often considered the holy grail of financial independence, refers to earnings generated with minimal effort or active involvement. One powerful avenue for generating passive income is dividend investingâ€"a strategy focused on building a portfolio of stocks that pay regular dividends. In this extensive exploration, we will unravel the concept of passive income, delve into the benefits of dividend investing, and outline strategies for constructing a portfolio that not only provides regular income streams but also fosters financial stability and long-term wealth growth.

Understanding Passive Income

Definition of Passive Income:

Passive income is income generated with little to no direct effort from the recipient. Unlike earned income from employment, passive income flows in without continuous active involvement, providing a degree of financial autonomy.

Sources of Passive Income:

1.   Dividend Income: Earnings from owning dividend-paying stocks.
2.   Rental Income: Revenue generated from owning and leasing real estate.
3.   Royalties: Payments for the use of intellectual property, such as books, music, or patents.
4.   Business Ownership: Earnings from businesses in which the owner has limited day-to-day involvement.

Benefits of Passive Income:

1.   Financial Freedom: Passive income can contribute to financial freedom by covering living expenses without the need for continuous work.
2.   Time Flexibility: Passive income streams allow for more flexibility in how one spends their time.
3.   Wealth Accumulation: Consistent passive income can contribute to long-term wealth accumulation and asset growth.

Dividend Investing: A Strategy for Passive Income

What is Dividend Investing:
Dividend investing involves building a portfolio of stocks from companies that distribute a portion of their earnings to shareholders in the form of dividends. These dividends provide investors with a regular stream of income.

Benefits of Dividend Investing:

1.   Stable Income: Dividend payments offer a stable and predictable source of income.
2.   Potential for Growth: Companies that consistently pay dividends often exhibit financial stability and long-term growth potential.
3.   Compounding Effect: Reinvesting dividends into additional shares can accelerate wealth accumulation through the compounding effect.
4.   Inflation Hedge: Dividend income may provide a hedge against inflation, as companies may increase dividend payments over time.

Building a Dividend-Focused Portfolio

Strategies for Constructing a Dividend Portfolio:

1.   Research and Selection: Conduct thorough research on companies with a history of stable dividend payments, strong financials, and growth potential.
2.   Diversification: Build a diversified portfolio across various sectors to reduce risk.
3.   Dividend Yield vs. Growth: Balance between high-dividend-yield stocks and those with the potential for dividend growth.
4.   Dividend Reinvestment Plans (DRIPs): Consider enrolling in DRIPs to automatically reinvest dividends in additional shares.
5.   Regular Portfolio Review: Periodically review and adjust the portfolio based on changing market conditions, company performance, and financial goals.

Risks and Challenges of Dividend Investing

Potential Risks:

1.   Economic Downturns: Economic challenges can impact a company's ability to maintain or increase dividend payments.
2.   Sector-specific Risks: Concentrating investments in specific sectors may expose the portfolio to industry-specific risks.
3.   Dividend Cuts: Companies may reduce or eliminate dividends during challenging times.
4.   Interest Rate Sensitivity: Rising interest rates can impact the attractiveness of dividend stocks.

Strategies for Mitigating Risks

1.   Diversification: Spread investments across different sectors and industries.
2.   Stress Testing: Assess how potential economic downturns might affect the portfolio and adjust accordingly.
3.   Research and Due Diligence: Regularly monitor the financial health of companies in the portfolio.
4.   Emergency Fund: Maintain an emergency fund to cover living expenses in case of a temporary reduction in dividend income.
5.   Regular Review: Periodically review and adjust the portfolio based on evolving market conditions and personal financial goals.

Passive Income Beyond Dividends

1. Real Estate Investment:

Rental Properties: Owning and leasing real estate for rental income.

2. Peer-to-Peer Lending:

Interest Income: Earning interest by lending money through online platforms.

3. Affiliate Marketing:

Commission Earnings: Promoting products or services and earning commissions on sales.

4. Digital Products:

Royalties: Creating and selling digital products, such as e-books, online courses, or software.

Conclusion

In conclusion, passive income, particularly through dividend investing, offers a pathway to financial independence and long-term wealth building. By constructing a well-researched and diversified dividend portfolio, investors can not only enjoy regular income streams but also benefit from the potential for capital appreciation over time. However, it's essential to acknowledge the associated risks and challenges and adopt strategies to mitigate them. Furthermore, considering other passive income streams beyond dividends can contribute to a more robust and diversified income-generating portfolio, ultimately fostering financial stability and sustained wealth growth.

Chapter 9: September -

Retirement Planning and Long-Term Financial Security
This chapter focuses on retirement planning, discussing the importance of early and consistent retirement savings, as well as the various retirement accounts and investment vehicles available to build long-term financial security.

Navigating the Path to Financial Security: A Comprehensive Guide to Retirement Planning

Retirement planning is a strategic and forward-thinking process that involves setting financial goals and creating a roadmap to ensure a comfortable and secure retirement. In this comprehensive exploration, we will delve into the significance of early and consistent retirement savings, examining the various retirement accounts and investment vehicles available to build long-term financial security.

The Importance of Early and Consistent Retirement Savings

1. Time as a Crucial Asset:

The power of compounding is amplified with time. Starting to save early allows your investments to grow exponentially over the years.

2. Mitigating the Impact of Market Volatility:

Consistent contributions enable investors to navigate market fluctuations more effectively, benefiting from dollar-cost averaging.

3. Building a Financial Safety Net:

Early savings create a robust financial safety net, offering flexibility and security during unforeseen circumstances.

4. Lifestyle Flexibility in Retirement:

Early and consistent savings provide the freedom to maintain or adjust lifestyle choices in retirement, ensuring a fulfilling post-working life.

Retirement Accounts: Vehicles for Long-Term Savings

1. 401(k) Plans:

Employer-sponsored retirement plans that allow employees to contribute a portion of their salary on a pre-tax basis. Potential for employer matching contributions, enhancing overall savings.

2. Individual Retirement Accounts (IRAs):

Personal retirement accounts with tax advantages, available in traditional and Roth formats.
Traditional IRAs offer tax-deferred growth, while Roth IRAs provide tax-free withdrawals in retirement.

3. Roth 401(k) Plans:

Combining features of Roth IRAs and traditional 401(k) plans, Roth 401(k)s offer tax-free withdrawals in retirement.

4. Pension Plans:

Employer-provided pension plans provide a fixed income stream in retirement based on years of service and salary.

5. Social Security:

A government-sponsored program providing a source of income during retirement based on a person's work history and contributions.

Investment Vehicles for Long-Term Growth

1. Stock Market Investments:

Equities offer the potential for high returns over the long term, providing growth for retirement portfolios. Diversification across different sectors and industries mitigates risk.

2. Bonds and Fixed-Income Investments:

Bonds provide stability and regular income through interest payments, acting as a counterbalance to the volatility of stocks.

3. Real Estate Investment:

Real estate can diversify a retirement portfolio, offering potential appreciation and rental income.

4. Mutual Funds:

   Investment vehicles that pool funds from multiple investors to invest in a diversified portfolio of stocks, bonds, or other securities.

5. Exchange-Traded Funds (ETFs):

Similar to mutual funds but traded on stock exchanges, providing diversification and flexibility.

Strategies for Long-Term Financial Security

1. Set Clear Retirement Goals:

Define specific retirement goals, considering lifestyle choices, healthcare needs, and potential travel or leisure activities.

2. Establish a Budget:

Create a realistic budget that aligns with retirement goals, accounting for living expenses, healthcare costs, and potential leisure activities.

3. Emergency Fund:

Maintain an emergency fund to cover unexpected expenses and avoid dipping into retirement savings during financial crises.

4. Regularly Review and Adjust:

Periodically review retirement goals, investment portfolios, and contributions to ensure alignment with evolving financial situations and market conditions.

5. Seek Professional Advice:

Consult financial advisors for personalized guidance on retirement planning, investment strategies, and tax implications.

Common Pitfalls in Retirement Planning

1. Insufficient Savings:

Failing to save enough for retirement can lead to financial stress during one's post-working years.

2. Ignoring Healthcare Costs:

Underestimating healthcare expenses in retirement can erode savings. Consider health insurance options and potential long-term care needs.

3. Overlooking Inflation:

Inflation can reduce the purchasing power of retirement savings over time. Factor in inflation when planning for future expenses.

4. Procrastination:

Delaying retirement planning can limit the effectiveness of compounding, making it harder to reach financial goals.

5. Underestimating Lifespan:

Plan for a longer lifespan to ensure financial security throughout retirement.

Tailoring Retirement Planning to Individual Needs

1. Early Career Planning:

Emphasize aggressive saving and investment strategies, taking advantage of the extended time horizon.

2. Mid-Career Adjustments:

Reevaluate retirement goals and adjust investment strategies based on changing circumstances, such as career advancements or family changes.

3. Pre-Retirement Preparations:

Fine-tune asset allocation, consider potential retirement income streams, and evaluate the timing of Social Security benefits.

4. Post-Retirement Financial Management:

Manage withdrawals strategically to ensure a steady income throughout retirement. Consider tax implications and potential legacy planning.

Conclusion

Retirement planning is a dynamic and personalized process that requires careful consideration, disciplined saving, and strategic investment. Recognizing the importance of early and consistent savings, leveraging diverse retirement accounts, and implementing a well-thought-out investment strategy are essential components for achieving long-term financial security. By navigating potential pitfalls, staying informed about financial options, and seeking professional advice when needed, individuals can embark on a journey towards a fulfilling and financially secure retirement.

Here's a detailed guide on the origin of gold, where to buy it, and how to store it:

The Origin of Gold

Gold, an element with the symbol Au on the periodic table, has a fascinating cosmic origin. It is created through the nuclear fusion processes that occur in the core of massive stars during their supernova explosions. These explosions release vast amounts of energy, scattering heavy elements like gold into space. Over billions of years, these elements accumulated to form celestial bodies, including our planet. Gold arrived on Earth through meteorite impacts, contributing to its presence in the Earth's crust.

Buying Gold

1. Local Dealers and Jewelers:
Visit local gold dealers or jewelers to purchase physical gold. Common forms include gold coins, bars, or jewelry.
Verify the authenticity and purity of the gold through reputable dealers.

2. Online Dealers:

Numerous online platforms facilitate the buying of gold. Reputable online dealers provide a wide range of gold products.
Ensure the platform has secure payment options and a transparent pricing structure.

3. Gold Exchanges:
Gold exchanges allow individuals to buy and sell gold like stocks. Examples include the New York Stock Exchange (NYSE) and the London Bullion Market (LBMA).

4. Gold Mining Stocks:

Investing in gold mining stocks provides exposure to the gold market without physically owning the metal.
Research mining companies, considering factors like production costs and exploration potential.

Storing Gold

1. Home Storage:
 Safe Deposit Box: Renting a safe deposit box at a bank offers a
 secure off-site storage option.
Home Safe: Installing a high-quality home safe adds an extra layer
of protection. However, it may not be as secure against professional
thieves.

2. Professional Storage:

Bullion Vault Storage Specialized companies provide secure vault
storage for your gold. This is a convenient option, but it comes
with storage fees.
Allocated vs. Unallocated Storage: Allocated storage means specific
gold bars are assigned to you, while unallocated storage means you
own a share of a pool of gold.

3. Digital Gold :

Gold ETFs (Exchange-Traded Funds): These financial instruments track
the gold price and don't involve physical possession.
 Digital Gold Platforms: Some platforms offer digital
 representations of physical gold, providing flexibility in buying
 and selling.

4. Legal Considerations

Tax Implications: Understand tax regulations related to buying,
selling, and storing gold in your jurisdiction. Consult with tax
professionals for accurate advice.

Documentation: Keep thorough records of your gold purchases,
including receipts, certificates of authenticity, and any relevant
transaction documentation.

5. Insurance

Homeowner's Insurance: If storing gold at home, ensure your
homeowner's insurance covers the value of your precious metals. This
may require additional coverage.

Storage Facility Insurance: If using a professional storage service,
inquire about their insurance policies. Verify the coverage details,
including potential exclusions.

6. Regular Audits and Appraisal's

Periodic Audits: If using professional storage, ensure the provider
conducts regular audits to verify the existence and authenticity of
your gold.

Appraisals: Periodic appraisals help assess the current value of your gold holdings. Consider engaging a certified appraiser for accuracy.

7. Security Measures

Home Security: Implement robust home security measures, including alarms, surveillance systems, and secure entry points.
Transportation Security: If personally transporting gold, use secure methods and avoid disclosing the contents to minimize the risk of theft.

13.   Selling Gold

Local Dealers: You can sell gold to local dealers or jewelers. Shop around for competitive prices.
Online Platforms: Explore online platforms that facilitate the selling of gold. Ensure they have reliable and secure mechanisms for transactions.

In conclusion, whether storing gold at home, in a safe deposit box, or with a professional storage service, thorough research, adherence to legal considerations, and proper security measures are crucial. Each storage method has its advantages and drawbacks, so choose based on your preferences, risk tolerance, and convenience. Remember, staying informed and seeking professional advice can significantly enhance your experience in buying, storing, and selling gold.

Chapter 10: October –

Harnessing the Potential of Technology in Investing
In October, we explore the latest financial tools and technologies that are transforming the investment landscape. From robo-advisors to algorithmic trading and fintech innovations, we discuss how technology can enhance investment strategies.

Transformative Technologies: Shaping the Future of Investments

In the ever-evolving landscape of finance, technological advancements are playing a pivotal role in reshaping how individuals and institutions approach investments. From the rise of robo-advisors to the complexities of algorithmic trading and the broader spectrum of fintech innovations, this comprehensive exploration delves into the latest financial tools and technologies that are transforming the investment landscape. Additionally, weâ€™ll discuss how technology is enhancing investment strategies, bringing new efficiencies, accessibility, and opportunities to investors worldwide.

The Rise of Robo-Advisors

Definition and Functionality:
Robo-advisors are automated, algorithm-driven platforms that provide
financial advice and investment management services. Leveraging
algorithms and mathematical models, these platforms offer cost-
effective and efficient solutions for investors.

Key Features:

1.   Automated Portfolio Management: Robo-advisors use
   algorithms to create and manage diversified portfolios
   tailored to individual risk tolerance and financial goals.
2.   Low Fees: Compared to traditional financial advisory
   services, robo-advisors often charge lower fees due to
   reduced human involvement.
3.   Accessibility: Robo-advisors make investment advice and
   management accessible to a broader audience, including
   novice investors.

Impact on Investment Landscape:

1.   Democratization of Investment Services: Robo-advisors
   have democratized access to investment advice, allowing
   individuals with varying levels of wealth to benefit from
   automated portfolio management.
2.   Personalization: Through advanced algorithms, robo-
   advisors can provide personalized investment strategies,
   taking into account individual risk preferences and
   financial objectives.

Algorithmic Trading: Navigating the Speed of Markets

Definition and Functionality:
Algorithmic trading involves the use of computer algorithms to
execute trades at speeds and frequencies that surpass human
capabilities. These algorithms analyze market data, identify
patterns, and execute trades based on predefined criteria.

Key Features:

1.   Speed and Efficiency: Algorithms can execute trades in
   milliseconds, taking advantage of market opportunities and
   minimizing latency.
2.   Risk Management: Algorithmic trading systems can
   incorporate risk management parameters to mitigate potential
   losses.
3.   Quantitative Analysis: Algorithms can analyze vast
   amounts of financial data to inform trading decisions,
   utilizing quantitative models and statistical analysis.

Impact on Investment Landscape:

1. Liquidity and Market Efficiency: Algorithmic trading contributes to market liquidity and efficiency by facilitating quick and precise transactions.
2. Reduced Trading Costs: The automation of trading processes can lead to reduced trading costs, as algorithms optimize execution prices.
3. Increased Trading Volumes: Algorithmic trading has contributed to higher trading volumes in financial markets.

Fintech Innovations: Beyond Traditional Boundaries

Definition and Diverse Applications:
Financial technology, or fintech, refers to the application of technology to improve and automate financial services. Fintech innovations span various areas, including payments, lending, blockchain, and crowdfunding.

Key Features:

1. Blockchain Technology: Providing decentralized and secure transactions through distributed ledger technology.
2. Digital Wallets and Payments: Facilitating seamless, contactless transactions through digital wallets and mobile payment solutions.
3. Peer-to-Peer Lending: Connecting borrowers directly with lenders, often through online platforms, bypassing traditional financial institutions.
4. Crowdfunding Platforms: Enabling individuals and businesses to raise capital from a large number of investors or donors.

Impact on Investment Landscape:

1. Financial Inclusion: Fintech innovations have expanded access to financial services, particularly in regions with limited traditional banking infrastructure.
2. Efficiency and Automation: Automation of financial processes through fintech solutions enhances efficiency, reduces costs, and minimizes manual errors.
3. Decentralization and Transparency: Blockchain technology promotes decentralization, transparency, and security in financial transactions.

Artificial Intelligence (AI) in Investment Strategies

Definition and Applications:
Artificial Intelligence involves the use of computer systems to perform tasks that typically require human intelligence. In the context of investments, AI is employed for data analysis, pattern recognition, and decision-making.

Key Features:

1.   Predictive Analytics: AI algorithms analyze historical and real-time data to make predictions about market trends and investment opportunities.
2.   Machine Learning: AI systems can adapt and improve over time by learning from data, enabling more accurate predictions and decision-making.
3.   Natural Language Processing (NLP): NLP allows AI systems to understand and analyze human language, facilitating the extraction of insights from news, social media, and other textual data.

Impact on Investment Landscape:

1.   Enhanced Decision-Making: AI assists investors in making more informed and data-driven decisions, reducing reliance on emotional reactions.
2.   Quantitative Analysis: AI algorithms excel at processing vast amounts of data, providing quantitative analysis that informs investment strategies.
3.   Risk Management: AI contributes to risk assessment and management by identifying potential risks and opportunities in real-time.

The Role of Big Data in Investment Analytics

Definition and Significance:
Big Data refers to the massive volume of structured and unstructured data generated by various sources. In investments, harnessing big data involves analyzing vast datasets to derive insights and inform decision-making.

Key Features:

1.   Data Aggregation: Big Data analytics aggregate information from diverse sources, including market data, economic indicators, and social media.
2.   Pattern Recognition: Analyzing large datasets helps identify patterns, correlations, and trends that may influence investment decisions.
3.   Real-Time Analysis: Big Data analytics enable real-time analysis of market conditions, providing investors with up-to-the-minute information.

Impact on Investment Landscape:

1.   Improved Forecasting: Big Data analytics contribute to more accurate forecasting of market trends, helping investors stay ahead of developments.
2.   Customized Investment Strategies: Analyzing individual investor data allows for the creation of personalized investment strategies aligned with specific goals and risk tolerance.

3.   Market Sentiment Analysis: Monitoring social media and news sentiment through big data analytics can offer insights into market sentiment and potential shifts.

Cybersecurity: Safeguarding Digital Assets

Significance of Cybersecurity in Finance:
As financial transactions and investment activities increasingly shift to digital platforms, ensuring the security of digital assets becomes paramount. Cybersecurity involves protecting systems, networks, and programs from digital attacks and unauthorized access.

Key Features:

1.   Data Encryption: Protecting sensitive financial information through encryption technologies.
2.   Multi-Factor Authentication: Enhancing security by requiring multiple forms of identification for access.
3.   Threat Detection Systems: Implementing systems that detect and respond to potential cybersecurity threats.

Impact on Investment Landscape:

1.   Protecting Investor Data: Cybersecurity measures safeguard investor data and prevent unauthorized access to sensitive information.
2.   Ensuring Transaction Security: Secure financial transactions are essential for maintaining trust in digital investment platforms.
3.   Mitigating Operational Risks: Cybersecurity measures reduce the risk of disruptions to financial operations due to cyberattacks.

Ethical Considerations and Regulatory Challenges

Ethical Considerations:

1.   Algorithmic Bias: The algorithms used in various financial technologies may exhibit biases, impacting investment decisions and perpetuating inequality.
2.   Privacy Concerns: The collection and use of vast amounts of personal data by fintech platforms raise privacy concerns, necessitating ethical data practices.
3.   Financial Inclusion: While fintech has expanded access to financial services, there are concerns about excluding certain demographics without access to digital technologies.

Regulatory Challenges

Chapter 11: November -

Sustainable and Ethical Investing for the Future
This chapter delves into the growing trend of sustainable and ethical investing. We discuss how investors can align their financial goals with their values by supporting companies with strong environmental, social, and governance (ESG) practices.

Navigating the Shift: Sustainable and Ethical Investing for the Future

The landscape of investing is undergoing a profound transformation as an increasing number of investors seek to align their financial goals with their values. This growing trend is epitomized by sustainable and ethical investing, where environmental, social, and governance (ESG) considerations play a pivotal role in investment decisions. In this comprehensive exploration, we will delve into the rationale behind the surge in sustainable and ethical investing, the key principles of ESG practices, and how investors can strategically align their financial goals with a commitment to sustainability.

The Evolution of Sustainable and Ethical Investing

Historical Context:
Sustainable and ethical investing has its roots in socially responsible investing (SRI), which emerged in the 1960s. Originally driven by ethical considerations, SRI sought to avoid investments in industries such as tobacco, alcohol, and weapons. Over time, the approach evolved to incorporate environmental and social factors, giving rise to the broader concept of ESG investing.

Rationale for the Surge:
1. Shifting Investor Values: Investors increasingly prioritize values-aligned investing, seeking to contribute to positive societal and environmental outcomes.
2. Risk Mitigation: Companies with strong ESG practices are viewed as more resilient and better equipped to navigate long-term risks, including regulatory changes and societal shifts.
3. Market Demand: Growing awareness of global challenges, such as climate change and social inequality, has led to increased demand for investments that address these issues.

Understanding ESG: Environmental, Social, and Governance Practices

1. Environmental (E):
Climate Change Impact: Assessing a company's carbon footprint, energy efficiency, and efforts to mitigate climate change.
Resource Efficiency: Evaluating sustainable resource management practices and waste reduction initiatives.
Renewable Energy Usage: Examining a company's reliance on renewable energy sources.

2. Social (S):
Labor Practices: Assessing fair labor practices, workplace diversity, and employee well-being.

Community Impact: Evaluating a company's contributions to local communities and social development initiatives.
 Product Safety:vEnsuring products and services adhere to safety standards and ethical production practices.

3. Governance (G):
Board Composition: Evaluating the diversity, independence, and competence of a company's board of directors.
Executive Compensation:** Examining fair and transparent executive compensation practices.
Corporate Governance Policies: Assessing the overall governance structure and policies in place.

 Strategies for Integrating ESG into Investment Decisions

1. Screening Strategies:
Positive Screening: Selecting investments based on specific ESG criteria aligned with positive values.
Negative Screening: Excluding investments that do not meet certain ethical or ESG standards, such as companies involved in controversial industries.

2. ESG Integration:
Systematically incorporating ESG factors into traditional financial analysis and decision-making processes.
Understanding how ESG considerations may impact a company's long-term performance and risk profile.

3. Thematic Investing:
Targeting specific themes, such as clean energy or social justice, to align investments with specific values or causes.
Investing in funds or companies that explicitly focus on addressing certain ESG challenges.

4. Engagement and Advocacy:
Active engagement with companies to encourage ESG improvements and positive changes in business practices.
Proxy voting and participation in shareholder resolutions to influence corporate behavior.

5. Impact Investing:
Investing with the intention of generating positive social or environmental impact alongside financial returns.
Focusing on measurable outcomes, such as reduced carbon emissions or improved community well-being.

Evaluating ESG Performance

1. ESG Ratings and Scores:
Various organizations provide ESG ratings and scores for companies based on their performance in environmental, social, and governance areas.
Investors can use these ratings to assess a company's overall ESG standing and make informed investment decisions.

2. ESG Reporting Standards:
Global reporting frameworks, such as the Global Reporting Initiative
(GRI) and the Sustainability Accounting Standards Board (SASB),
provide standardized ESG reporting guidelines.
Companies adhering to these standards enhance transparency and
comparability of their ESG practices.

3. Industry-Specific Considerations:
Recognizing that ESG factors may vary by industry, investors should
consider sector-specific nuances when evaluating performance.
Understanding the unique environmental and social impacts associated
with specific industries.

The Financial Case for ESG Investing

1. Long-Term Performance:
Studies suggest that companies with strong ESG practices may exhibit
better long-term financial performance.
Reduced exposure to risks related to environmental and social issues
can contribute to sustained profitability.

2. Risk Mitigation:
ESG factors can serve as indicators of potential risks, including
regulatory, repetitional, and operational risks.
Companies with robust ESG practices are better positioned to
navigate unforeseen challenges.

3. Access to Capital:
Investors increasingly consider ESG factors when making investment
decisions, leading to greater capital allocation to companies with
strong ESG credentials.
Access to sustainable and green financing options may enhance a
company's overall financial resilience.

4. Attraction of Millennial Investors:
Millennials, a significant demographic in the investor landscape,
are more likely to prioritize investments aligned with their values.
ESG considerations cater to the preferences of this generation,
influencing capital flows.

Challenges and Criticisms

1. Lack of Standardization:
The absence of standardized ESG metrics and reporting practices
poses challenges for consistent evaluation.
Investors may face difficulties in comparing ESG performance across
companies and industries.

2. Greenwashing Concerns:
Some companies may engage in "greenwashing," presenting a misleading
picture of their environmental or social practices.

Investors need to exercise diligence in verifying the authenticity
of ESG claims.

3. Trade-Offs with Financial Returns:
Critics argue that prioritizing ESG considerations may lead to
trade-offs with financial returns.
Investors must carefully balance their values with their financial
objectives.

4. Limited Impact Measurement:
Measuring the tangible impact of ESG investments on specific
environmental or social outcomes can be challenging.
Investors may seek clearer methodologies for gauging the
effectiveness of their impact investments.

Future Trends in Sustainable and Ethical Investing

1. Regulatory Developments:
The integration of ESG considerations into regulatory frameworks is
likely to increase, promoting standardized reporting practices.
Regulatory support may encourage more companies to adopt and
disclose comprehensive ESG strategies.

2. Technological Innovations:
Advancements in technology, including artificial intelligence and
big data analytics, may enhance ESG data collection and analysis.
Technological tools can provide investors with more accurate and
timely information for decision-making.

3. Global Collaboration:
International collaboration among governments, organizations, and
investors is anticipated to grow, fostering a unified approach to
addressing global challenges through sustainable and ethical
investing.
Global standards and frameworks may emerge to facilitate cross-
border ESG investments and align practices on a broader scale.

4. Evolution of Impact Measurement:
As the demand for impact investing rises, there is likely to be a
focus on developing more sophisticated methodologies for measuring
and quantifying the social and environmental impact of investments.
Standardized impact metrics could become more prevalent, offering
investors clearer insights into the outcomes of their sustainable
investments.

5. Increased Corporate Accountability:
Growing awareness and activism around ESG issues are likely to lead
to increased corporate accountability.
Shareholder activism and engagement may push companies to adopt and
strengthen their ESG practices.

Practical Steps for Investors

1. Clarify Values and Objectives:

Define personal values and investment objectives to guide the selection of ESG criteria.
Consider whether the focus is on environmental conservation, social justice, governance practices, or a combination of these factors.

2. Research and Due Diligence:
Conduct thorough research on companies and investment products to assess their ESG performance.
Leverage ESG ratings, reports, and third-party assessments to inform investment decisions.

3. Diversify ESG Investments:
Diversify across various sectors and industries to spread ESG investments and manage risk.
Consider both established ESG leaders and emerging companies with strong sustainability initiatives.

4. Engage and Advocate:
 Engage with companies through shareholder activism or proxy voting to advocate for improved ESG practices.
Support initiatives that align with ESG values and participate in dialogues that promote positive change.

5. Stay Informed:
Stay abreast of evolving ESG trends, regulatory changes, and advancements in sustainable and ethical investing.
Continuously reassess and adjust investment strategies based on emerging opportunities and challenges.

6. Work with Financial Advisors:
Consult with financial advisors who specialize in sustainable investing to receive tailored guidance.
Financial professionals can provide insights into ESG strategies, risks, and potential returns.

Conclusion

Sustainable and ethical investing is no longer a niche concept but a mainstream approach that reflects the evolving values and priorities of investors. As the demand for ESG-aligned investments continues to rise, companies are under increasing pressure to adopt responsible business practices. The integration of ESG considerations into investment strategies provides an avenue for individuals to contribute to positive societal and environmental change while pursuing their financial goals.

While the trend towards sustainable investing is promising, challenges such as standardization issues and greenwashing concerns must be addressed to maintain credibility and trust in the market. Investors, corporations, and regulators play crucial roles in shaping the future of sustainable and ethical investing. As the field continues to evolve, it is essential for all stakeholders to collaborate, innovate, and remain committed to building a more sustainable and responsible global financial ecosystem. In doing so,

investors can not only achieve their financial objectives but also
contribute to a more sustainable and equitable future for
generations to come.

Chapter 12: December -

 Reflecting on the Year and Planning for the Future
In December, we reflect on the year's financial decisions and
outcomes, and we lay the groundwork for the year ahead. We emphasize
the importance of continuous learning, adaptation, and long-term
financial planning as key components of wealth building

Reflecting on Financial Decisions: A Comprehensive Guide to Year-End
Review

As the year draws to a close, it's an opportune time to engage in a
thorough reflection on your financial decisions and outcomes. This
comprehensive guide will walk you through the process of evaluating
the past year and lay the groundwork for a financially successful
year ahead. Emphasizing continuous learning, adaptation, and long-
term financial planning, we'll explore key components that
contribute to wealth building based on the factors we've discussed.

I. Evaluating Financial Goals and Achievements

1. Reviewing Your Financial Goals:
Assess the goals you set at the beginning of the year.
Identify which goals were achieved, partially achieved, or not met.

2. Celebrating Achievements:
Acknowledge and celebrate the financial milestones and achievements
you reached during the year.
Recognize the progress made towards long-term objectives.

3. Analyzing Unmet Goals:
Understand the reasons behind unmet goals. Was it due to external
factors, lack of planning, or unforeseen circumstances?
Consider whether certain goals need to be adjusted or realigned for
the upcoming year.

II. Assessing Income and Expenses

1. Income Review:
Examine your sources of income throughout the year.
Evaluate whether there are opportunities to diversify or increase
income streams.

2. Expense Analysis:
Break down your spending into categories to identify major areas of
expenditure.

Assess whether spending aligns with priorities and if there are
areas to cut back or optimize.

3. Budget Evaluation:
Review your budget and compare it with actual spending.
Adjust your budget for the upcoming year based on insights gained
from this analysis.

III. Investment Portfolio Review

1. Portfolio Performance:
Evaluate the performance of your investment portfolio over the past
year.
Assess how individual assets contributed to overall portfolio
growth.

2. Risk Tolerance and Asset Allocation:
Reassess your risk tolerance and ensure that your asset allocation
aligns with your financial goals.
Consider rebalancing your portfolio if necessary.

3. Learning from Market Trends:
Reflect on market trends and how they influenced your investments.
Identify areas where your investment strategy aligned well with
market conditions and where adjustments might be needed.

IV. Debt Management and Credit Review

1. Debt Repayment Analysis:
Evaluate progress in repaying any outstanding
debts.
Consider prioritizing high-interest debts and explore strategies for
accelerated repayment.

2. Credit Score Check:
Review your credit score and credit report.
Address any discrepancies and implement strategies to improve your
credit health.

3. Avoiding Accumulation of New Debt:
Assess whether you've been successful in avoiding the accumulation
of new debt.
Establish strategies to maintain responsible borrowing habits in the
upcoming year.

V. Emergency Fund and Insurance Review

1. Emergency Fund Evaluation:
 Review the status of your emergency fund.
 Ensure that it aligns with your current financial situation and
 provides an adequate safety net.

2. Insurance Coverage Check:

Evaluate your insurance coverage, including life, health, and property insurance.
Consider whether adjustments are needed based on changes in your circumstances.

3. Planning for Contingencies:
Identify potential financial risks and develop contingency plans.
Ensure that your emergency fund and insurance coverage provide sufficient protection.

VI. Tax Planning and Strategy Assessment.

1. Tax Documents and Records:
Organize tax-related documents and records.
Prepare for tax season by ensuring that all necessary information is readily available.

2. Tax Efficiency Assessment:
Evaluate the tax efficiency of your investments and overall financial strategy.
Explore opportunities for tax optimization in the coming year.

3. Capitalizing on Tax-Advantaged Accounts:
Maximize contributions to tax-advantaged accounts, such as retirement and health savings accounts.
Ensure that you're taking full advantage of available tax benefits.

VII. Continuous Learning and Adaptation

1. Reflecting on Financial Knowledge:
Assess your understanding of financial concepts and investment strategies.
Identify areas where you can deepen your knowledge.

2. Staying Informed about Market Trends:
Commit to staying informed about economic trends, market developments, and financial news.
Subscribe to reputable financial publications and follow reliable sources for updates.

3. Networking and Professional Advice:
Engage with financial communities and networks to share insights and learn from others.
Consider seeking professional advice for specific financial aspects, especially those outside your expertise.

VIII. Long-Term Financial Planning

1. Reassessing Long-Term Goals:
Reflect on your long-term financial goals and whether they need adjustments.
Consider how life changes and evolving priorities impact your overarching financial plan.

2. Retirement Planning Review:
Evaluate the progress of your retirement savings and investment strategy.
Consider whether adjustments are needed to meet retirement goals.

3. Estate Planning and Legacy Considerations:
Review your estate planning documents and beneficiaries.
Consider how your financial decisions align with your legacy goals and family considerations.

IX. Setting Financial Resolutions for the Year Ahead

1. SMART Goals Setting:
Establish SMART (Specific, Measurable, Achievable, Relevant, Time-bound) financial goals for the upcoming year.
Ensure that each goal is clearly defined and aligned with your broader financial vision.

2. Creating Action Plans:
Develop actionable steps and plans to achieve each financial goal.
Break down larger goals into smaller, manageable tasks with specific deadlines.

3. Prioritizing Financial Wellness:
Consider financial wellness as a holistic approach to overall well-being.
Incorporate physical, mental, and emotional well-being into your financial resolutions.

X. Implementing Systems for Financial Tracking

1. Financial Tracking Tools:
Explore and utilize financial tracking tools and apps.
Automate processes where possible to streamline budgeting, expense tracking, and investment monitoring.

2. Regular Check-Ins:
Schedule regular check-ins throughout the year to assess progress toward financial goals.
Adjust strategies as needed based on changing circumstances or unexpected challenges.

3. Accountability Partners:
Consider having an accountability partner, whether a friend, family member, or financial advisor.
Regularly share progress and challenges, fostering a sense of responsibility and support.

XI. Cultivating a Mindset of Financial Empowerment

1. Positive Financial Mindset

Cultivate a positive financial mindset that embraces challenges as opportunities for growth.
Shift from a scarcity mindset to an abundance mindset, focusing on possibilities and proactive financial management.

2. Learning from Mistakes:
View financial mistakes as learning experiences rather than failures.
Identify lessons from past decisions and use them to make more informed choices in the future.

3. Embracing Adaptability:
Acknowledge the dynamic nature of personal finances and embrace adaptability.
Be open to adjusting goals, strategies, and plans based on changing circumstances and new opportunities.

XII. Incorporating Mindful Spending and Lifestyle Choices

1. Mindful Spending Practices:
Practice mindful spending by aligning purchases with values and priorities.
Prioritize experiences and items that bring lasting joy and fulfillment.

2. Assessing Lifestyle Choices:
Consider how lifestyle choices impact overall financial well-being.
Evaluate whether adjustments to lifestyle can contribute to increased savings and financial resilience.

3. Sustainable and Ethical Consumption:
Embrace sustainable and ethical consumption practices.
Support companies that align with your values and contribute positively to environmental and social causes.

XIII. Reviewing Legal and Financial Documentation.

1. Legal Document Check:
Review legal documents such as wills, trusts, and powers of attorney.
Ensure that these documents reflect your current wishes and circumstances.

2. Beneficiary Updates:
Check and update beneficiaries on financial accounts and insurance policies.
Confirm that designations align with your intentions and family considerations.

3. Document Organization:
Establish a system for organizing financial documents and statements.
Ensure easy access to important information, especially in case of emergencies.

XIV. Reflecting on Financial Well-Being Holistically.

1. Holistic Well-Being Assessment:
Evaluate financial well-being as part of a broader holistic
assessment.
Consider how financial health intersects with physical, mental, and
emotional well-being.

2. Balance and Harmony:
Strive for balance and harmony in your financial life.
Avoid overemphasizing one aspect of your finances at the expense of
others.

3. Seeking Professional Guidance:
Consider consulting with financial professionals, including
financial advisors and planners.
Leverage their expertise to optimize your financial strategy and
address specific challenges.

XV. Gratitude and Reflection on Achievements.

1. Expressing Gratitude:
Take a moment to express gratitude for the opportunities and
achievements of the past year.
Acknowledge the positive aspects of your financial journey.

2. Learning from Challenges:
Reflect on challenges faced and the resilience displayed in
overcoming them.
Identify lessons learned and personal growth achieved through
financial challenges.

3. Setting Gratitude Intentions:
Incorporate gratitude into your financial intentions for the
upcoming year.
Cultivate an attitude of appreciation for the resources and
opportunities available.

XVI. Leveraging Technology for Financial Management

1. Digital Budgeting and Tracking:
Explore digital tools for budgeting, expense tracking, and financial
planning.
Utilize apps and platforms that streamline financial management
processes.

2. Automation for Savings and Investments:
Automate savings contributions and investment transactions to ensure
consistency.
Take advantage of features like automatic transfers and
contributions.

3. Cybersecurity Measures:

Implement cybersecurity measures to protect sensitive financial
information.
Regularly update passwords and employ two-factor authentication for
added security.

XVII. Collaboration and Shared Financial Goals

1. Collaborative Decision-Making:
Involve family members or partners in financial discussions and
decision-making.
Ensure alignment in financial goals and work together towards shared
objectives.

2. Regular Financial Updates:
 Schedule regular financial updates with family members or partners.
Maintain open communication about financial challenges, goals, and
achievements.

3. Teaching Financial Literacy:
 If applicable, engage in teaching financial literacy to children or
 family members.
Install a foundational understanding of money management principles.

XVIII. Monitoring Economic and Market Trends

1. Economic Awareness:
Stay informed about broader economic trends that may impact personal
finances.
Understand how macroeconomic factors influence your financial
landscape.

2. Investment Opportunities:
Keep an eye on emerging investment opportunities and market trends.
Be open to adjusting your investment strategy based on evolving
market conditions.

3. Networking and Insights:
Engage with financial communities, both online and offline.
Leverage insights from discussions and networking opportunities to
enhance financial decision-making.

XIX. Conclusion: Embracing a Holistic Approach to Financial Well-
Being

In conclusion, reflecting on the year's financial decisions and
outcomes is a powerful practice that lays the groundwork for a
successful and fulfilling financial future. By embracing continuous
learning, adapting to changing circumstances, and incorporating
long-term financial planning, individuals can navigate the
complexities of wealth building.

The importance of holistic well-being cannot be overstated.
Balancing financial goals with mindful spending, ethical choices,
and a positive mindset

Bonus Points on crypto Trading in a Bull Market

In a crypto bull market, navigating the surge in enthusiasm and prices requires a strategic approach. Here's a comprehensive summary covering key aspects to consider:

1. Market Research and Education
    - Start by understanding the crypto market fundamentals.
    - Research various projects, their use cases, and technology.
    - Stay updated on market trends, news, and regulatory developments.
    - Educate yourself on technical analysis for better decision-making.

2. Portfolio Diversification
    - Diversify your crypto holdings across different assets to manage risk.
    - Consider a mix of established and promising but riskier projects.
    - Allocate based on your risk tolerance and investment goals.

    4.   Risk Management
    - Set clear risk parameters and stick to them.
    - Use tools like stop-loss orders to limit potential losses.
    - Avoid investing more than you can afford to lose.

4. Profit-Taking Strategies
    - Develop a profit-taking plan to capitalize on gains.
    - Consider taking partial profits at predefined price levels.
    - Reinvest profits strategically or diversify further.

5. Stay Informed on Regulatory Changes
    - Keep abreast of regulatory developments globally.
    - Understand the impact of regulations on different crypto assets.
    - Adjust your strategy based on regulatory shifts.

6. Security Measures
    - Strengthen security measures for your crypto holdings.
    - Use hardware wallets for long-term storage.
    - Be cautious about sharing sensitive information.

7. Stay Emotionally Disciplined
    - Emotions can drive impulsive decisions; stay disciplined.
    - Avoid FOMO (Fear of Missing Out) and FUD (Fear, Uncertainty, Doubt).
    - Stick to your investment plan regardless of market sentiment.

8. Leverage and Margin Trading Caution
    - Exercise caution with leverage and margin trading.
    - Understand the risks involved and potential liquidation scenarios.

- Consider avoiding leverage if you're not experienced.

9. Monitoring and Adjusting
    - Regularly monitor your portfolio and market conditions.
    - Be ready to adjust your strategy based on changing trends.
    - Keep an eye on macroeconomic factors influencing the market.

10. Building a Support Network
    - Engage with the crypto community for insights and discussions.
    - Join forums, attend meetups, and participate in social media.
    - Exchange ideas and experiences with other investors.

11. Tax Planning
    - Understand tax implications of crypto gains in your jurisdiction.
    - Keep detailed records of transactions for accurate reporting.
    - Consult with tax professionals for advice.

12. Long-Term Perspective
    - While navigating short-term gains, maintain a long-term perspective.
    - Identify projects with lasting value and potential for future growth.
    - Don't be swayed by short-term market fluctuations.

13. Preparing for Market Corrections
    - Anticipate and prepare for market corrections.
    - Have a strategy for buying the dip and accumulating during downturns.
    - Stay focused on the long-term potential of your investments.

14. Exit Strategy
    - Plan your exit strategy based on your financial goals.
    - Gradually cash out profits according to your predefined plan.
    - Reassess your portfolio periodically.

15. Continuous Learning and Adaptation
    - The crypto landscape evolves rapidly; be open to learning.
    - Adapt your strategy based on new technologies and market dynamics.
    - Stay curious and explore emerging opportunities.

In conclusion, a successful approach to a crypto bull market involves a combination of research, disciplined decision-making, risk management, and adaptability. Continuous learning and a long-term perspective are crucial for sustained success in the dynamic crypto space.

Here's a list of some popular crypto trading platforms and apps:

1.   Binance
2.   Coinbase
3.   Kraken

4.   Gemini
5.   Bitstamp
6.   Huobi
7.   KuCoin
8.   OKEx
9.   eToro
10.   Crypto.com

Regarding Crypto.com, you can use the referral link https://crypto.com/app/n8rk2y7q67 to sign up and both you and the person who referred you will receive $25 USD. It's a great way to benefit from mutual referrals. Happy trading!

How do I keep my crypto safe?

To keep your crypto safe, use reputable wallets, enable two-factor authentication, keep private keys offline, regularly update software, be cautious with online activities, and consider hardware wallets for added security.

Here's a list on how to keep your Cryptocurrency safe and secure.

1. Use reputable wallets: Choose well-established wallets with a track record of security.
2. Enable two-factor authentication (2FA): Add an extra layer of security to your accounts.
3. Keep private keys offline: Use hardware wallets or paper wallets to store private keys securely.
4. Regularly update software: Keep your wallet software and devices up to date to patch vulnerabilities.
5. Be cautious online: Avoid suspicious links, phishing attempts, and only use secure networks for transactions.
6. Backup your wallet: Keep multiple secure backups of your wallet's recovery phrase or private keys.
7. Diversify storage: Consider spreading your crypto holdings across different wallets and storage methods.
8. Use secure connections: Make sure your internet connection is secure, especially when accessing wallets.
9. Keep a low profile: Avoid sharing details of your crypto holdings publicly to minimize the risk of targeted attacks.
10. Research projects: Before investing, thoroughly research and choose reputable cryptocurrencies and projects.

Remember, the key is a combination of cautious online behavior, secure storage methods, and staying informed about potential risks in the crypto space.

If you've made it this far, congratulations — you're now among the 1% armed with the knowledge to unlock your financial freedom. Share the wealth of insights from "Rich Decisions: A Year of Financial Wisdom" with your family and friends, because financial empowerment is a journey best shared.

Remember, mindset is the key to everything. Cultivate a winning mindset that extends beyond finances, influencing every facet of your life. As you apply these principles, don't forget to connect and share your journey with me on Instagram @monie_gad. Let's inspire others to embark on their path to financial success and a life filled with abundance. Your journey is just beginning, and together, we can create a community dedicated to making rich decisions in every area of life. Cheers to your prosperous future!

My Personal Story Driving to Success: A Journey from Rideshare to $100,000

Introduction: Unveiling the Road Ahead

In the vibrant tapestry of urban life, where the rhythm of the city echoes through its streets, my journey with Uber unfoldedâ€"a journey marked by determination, resilience, and the unmistakable hum of the rideshare engine. Picture yourself in the driverâ€™s seat as I take you through the labyrinth of highs, lows, and unexpected turns that shaped my quest to reach the coveted milestone of earning $100,000 with Uber.

The city, ever awake and alive, became both my canvas and my companion as I embarked on this odyssey. From the break of dawn to the stillness of the night, the hustle and bustle of the urban landscape became my backdrop, and the stories etched in every ride became my narrative.

Engaging Visual: Imagine a captivating image that encapsulates the essence of rideshare drivingâ€"a snapshot of a bustling cityscape illuminated by the glow of headlights and the vibrant trails of tail lights. Cars in motion, weaving through the streets, tell the story of countless journeysâ€"a powerful visual symbolizing the heartbeat of rideshare life.

As I share my experiences, envision yourself navigating through these city streets, each ride a unique chapter in the larger tale of my pursuit. Join me as I traverse the urban jungle, where every street corner holds a potential adventure and every passenger brings a story of their own.

The streets, lined with possibilities, became my workplace, and the hum of the rideshare engine, my daily anthem. Together, weâ€™ll explore the peaks of success, the valleys of challenges, and the unexpected twists that defined this remarkable expedition.

Engaging Visual: Transition seamlessly from the initial cityscape image to a snapshot of a driverâ€™s perspectiveâ€"a view from behind the wheel, capturing the essence of the road, the dashboard, and the anticipation of the next ride.

As we navigate through the upcoming chapters, let this introduction serve as your ticket to the front seat of my rideshare journeyâ€"an immersive experience into the world where determination fuels the

drive, and the journey is as important as the destination. So buckle
up, for the engine is revving, and the road awaits.

Chapter 1: The Daily Drive - Unveiling the Routine

In the predawn hush, the blare of the alarm marks the commencement
of each day. Stepping into the driver's seat, I invite you to peer
into the intricacies of my daily routine—a routine woven with the
threads of determination and honed by the discipline that became the
driving force behind my journey to a $100,000 milestone with Uber.

As the sun begins its ascent, so does my dedication to strategically
selecting routes that promise not only a flurry of rides but also a
cascade of earnings. The Uber app, my trusty navigator, reveals a
digital tapestry of busy routes and high-demand areas that set the
stage for a day in the life of a rideshare driver.

Engaging Visual: Picture a series of screenshots from the Uber app,
capturing the dynamic landscape of busy routes and areas teeming
with high-demand icons. These visual snippets offer a glimpse into
the calculated decisions made at the start of each day, illustrating
the synergy between technology and strategy.

The journey unfolds, not just in miles, but in the subtle cadence of
consistency. Embracing the importance of repeating the ritual, day
in and day out, proved to be the cornerstone of my success. The
daily routine, meticulously crafted, became a ritual that harnessed
the power of consistency, paving the way for remarkable achievements
on the road.

Personal Anecdote: However, the road to success was not without its
bumps—sometimes quite literally. Navigate with me through the
challenges of traffic violation tickets and encounters with police
officers seemingly driven by monthly quotas. In these moments, the
fines and stops were not just monetary setbacks but lessons etched
into the journey, teaching resilience in the face of unexpected
detours.

The hum of the rideshare engine became a symphony of both triumphs
and tribulations, with traffic lights as notes and city streets as
the stage. Through these challenges, the importance of staying the
course, even when faced with unforeseen obstacles, became a guiding
principle.

The daily routine was not merely a schedule but a rhythmic dance
with the city—a choreography of choices, risks, and rewards. Join
me in the next chapter as we delve deeper into the financial
intricacies of this dance, exploring the income breakdown that
mirrored the beats of my rideshare journey.

Chapter 2: Counting the Miles - Income Breakdown

In the world of rideshare, success is measured not just in miles covered but in the dollars earned with each journey. Join me as we pull back the financial curtain, taking a closer look at the intricate dance of income and expenses that unfolded during my pursuit of a $100,000 milestone with Uber.

As the odometer ticks and the earnings roll in, understanding the nuances of income breakdown becomes paramount. Itâ€™s not just about the fares collected but the detailed calculations that painted a clearer picture of the financial tapestry woven on the streets.

Engaging Visual: Imagine a series of charts and graphs, each telling a story of income trends, expenses, and the ebb and flow of challenges on the overall earnings. Witness the peaks and valleys, understanding the impact of traffic tickets, unexpected stops, and the resilience that kept the income graph on an upward trajectory.

Every mile covered is a mile earned, but it is the unexpected discoveries in these financial calculations that transformed a simple drive into a lucrative venture. Uncover the surprising elements that added substantial digits to the income column, proving that success often lies in the details.

Personal Challenge: Yet, the road to financial triumph was not without its share of potholes. Share the emotional rollercoaster of dealing with accidentsâ€"a stark reminder that the road, as promising as it may be, is not immune to unexpected detours. The struggles faced in replacing two cars echo not only in the screech of metal against metal but also in the emotional toll it exacted.

These challenges, like unexpected toll booths, slowed the pace but never halted the journey. Instead, they became lessons etched into the journey, teaching not just resilience but also the art of adapting to unforeseen circumstances on the rideshare highway.

As the financial puzzle pieces fell into place, the income breakdown revealed more than just numbersâ€"it uncovered the resilience and determination that fueled the drive. The financial rollercoaster mirrored the highs and lows of the road, creating a narrative where challenges became stepping stones rather than roadblocks.

In the next chapter, we transition from the financial intricacies to the strategic decisions that defined my journey. Explore the tips and tricks that turned each ride into an opportunity for success, and witness the transformation from a driver navigating the streets to a navigator mastering the art of rideshare.

Chapter 3: Navigating Success - Tips for Aspiring Drivers

In the intricate maze of rideshare driving, success isnâ€™t just about the journey; itâ€™s about the strategic choices made along the way. Join me as we navigate the twists and turns, uncovering the secrets that transformed each ride into an opportunity for success and propelled me towards earning $100,000 with Uber.

The road to success isn't a straight line—it's a series of calculated turns and strategic moves that define a driver's trajectory. Explore with me the art of positioning oneself for success, beginning with the ideal spots for different times of the day.

Engaging Visual: Picture detailed map overlays, where optimal driving routes intertwine with high-demand areas. These visual guides unveil the strategic decisions that transformed ordinary rides into lucrative opportunities, highlighting the importance of adapting to the dynamic landscape of rideshare driving.

In the daily quest for success, each ride is an opportunity to make strategic choices. Whether it's the morning rush hour, the evening commute, or the nightlife frenzy, understanding the nuances of ideal driving spots became the compass guiding my journey.

Personal Challenge: The road to success, however, isn't always paved smoothly. Reflect with me on the lessons learned from overcoming obstacles and setbacks. The challenges faced weren't roadblocks but rather stepping stones, emphasizing the resilience and determination that turned detours into opportunities.

Chapter 4: Safety First - Measures for a Secure Ride

In the realm of rideshare driving, safety isn't just a passenger's expectation; it's a driver's commitment to ensuring every journey is secure. Join me as we delve into the crucial measures that prioritize safety on the rideshare highway, transforming each ride into a secure and reliable experience.

Safety measures are the seatbelt of the rideshare journey—an essential aspect that ensures a smooth and secure ride for both drivers and passengers. It begins with the installation of security tools, such as cameras that act as vigilant guardians during every mile traveled.

Engaging Visual: Visualize a series of images showcasing safety tools—a collage of dash cams, inside-car cameras, and suggested safety features that empower drivers to create a secure environment. These tools not only act as witnesses to the journey but also as deterrents against untoward incidents.

However, safety goes beyond the tangible tools—it's about the mindset and actions of the driver. Personal experiences become the compass in navigating challenging situations, ensuring composure during unexpected turns in the journey.

Personal Anecdote: Share intimate stories of maintaining composure in challenging situations, where every decision made was a step towards ensuring the safety of both passengers and the driver. These anecdotes illuminate the importance of staying calm amidst the storm, proving that a steady hand on the wheel is not just a metaphor but a commitment to safety.

Handling challenging situations isn't just about reacting—it's about proactively creating an environment where safety is paramount. From acknowledging the importance of maintaining composure to understanding the potential risks, this chapter unfolds as a guide to fostering a secure rideshare experience.

In the final chapter, we shift gears from safety measures to the broader aspect of professionalism—a crucial component that not only enhances the rideshare experience but also contributes to the success and reputation of the driver. Join me as we explore the importance of personal presentation, maintaining professionalism, and the role it plays in elevating the journey from a simple ride to a memorable experience.

Chapter 5: Beyond the Horizon - Maintaining Professionalism

As the rideshare journey extends beyond the road, a driver's professionalism becomes the compass guiding each interaction. Join me as we explore the significance of personal presentation and delve into the realm where grooming tips and a spotless vehicle elevate the rideshare experience from a mere drive to a polished journey.

Professionalism is the unseen force that not only propels a driver's success but also shapes the very fabric of the rideshare experience. In this chapter, we'll unravel the elements that contribute to professionalism, beginning with the tangible aspects of personal presentation.

From the moment a passenger steps into the vehicle, they become part of an experience woven with professionalism. Grooming tips, from a proper lineup to a well-groomed beard, are the brushstrokes that paint a picture of a driver committed to excellence.

Engaging Visual: Witness the transformation with before-and-after images—a visual journey that captures the essence of a well-groomed driver and a spotless rideshare vehicle. These images serve as a testament to the commitment to professionalism, where the vehicle becomes a reflection of the driver's dedication to providing a premium service.

Professionalism is not just about appearance; it's about the conduct that accompanies it. Narrate memorable moments and challenges faced with passengers, underscoring the role of maintaining professionalism in the face of varying circumstances. Each interaction becomes an opportunity to showcase a commitment to excellence, leaving a lasting impression on passengers.

Personal Anecdote: Share personal stories that highlight the challenges faced and memorable moments experienced, emphasizing the importance of maintaining professionalism. Whether itâ€™s a heartwarming encounter or a situation that tested composure, these anecdotes illustrate that professionalism is the linchpin that transforms a ride into an experience.

As we conclude this journey, professionalism emerges as the bridge connecting the driverâ€™s commitment to excellence and the passengerâ€™s expectation of a reliable, safe, and enjoyable ride. In the final chapter, letâ€™s weave all these elements together, emphasizing the holistic approach that transforms a rideshare driver from a mere navigator to a memorable experience curator.

Conclusion: The Road Traveled and the Journey Ahead

As we bring this journey to a close, reflect with me on the miles covered, the challenges overcome, and the transformative power of the rideshare highway. Success, in the world of rideshare driving, is not just about reaching a destinationâ€"itâ€™s about embracing the entire journey, every twist, every turn, and every unexpected detour.

The road behind us is marked with the echoes of determination and the hum of the rideshare engine, resonating as a testament to what can be achieved with grit, resilience, and a dash of positivity. This journey, from the pre-dawn alarm to the final drop-off, is not just about the dollars earned but the lessons learned, the obstacles overcome, and the personal growth experienced at every turn.

Engaging Visual: Picture a powerful imageâ€"an embodiment of achievement and success. Perhaps itâ€™s a snapshot of a driver, arms raised in triumph, celebrating with a satisfied passenger who symbolizes the journeyâ€™s purpose and the lives touched along the way. This visual serves as a reminder that success isnâ€™t just measured in dollars but in the smiles exchanged and the connections forged.

As we part ways, I leave you with a final push of motivation. Your own rideshare adventures await, and the highway is open for you to navigate. Remember, success isnâ€™t a singular destinationâ€"itâ€™s the accumulation of every mile, every challenge faced, and every lesson learned. Embrace the journey in its entirety, for it is in the journey that you discover not just the destination, but the strength within yourself.

Closing Thoughts: I Encourage readers to carry with them the lessons learned from this journeyâ€"a commitment to determination, discipline, and a positive attitude. These qualities are the fuel that propels not just a rideshare vehicle but also the aspirations and dreams of those at the wheel.

In the unpredictable world of rideshare driving, every ride is an opportunity, every challenge a chance for growth, and every journey a canvas waiting to be painted with determination and resilience. Embrace the road ahead with an open heart, a focused mind, and the unwavering belief that, just like the driver who turned a simple ride into a $100,000 milestone, you too have the power to transform your rideshare adventure into a transformative journey of success.

The engine is revving, the road awaits—may your rideshare adventures be filled with prosperity, fulfillment, and the joy of a journey well-traveled. Safe travels, fellow navigator, and may your road be paved with success and satisfaction.

Bonus Section: Navigating Uber Surge Pricing

Navigating through Uber surge pricing is like maneuvering through a dynamic landscape, and understanding how it works can be the key to making the most out of these peak demand moments.

How Surge Pricing Works:

1. Demand for Rides Increases:
There are instances when the demand for rides skyrockets due to factors such as bad weather, rush hour, or special events. During these times, the sheer number of ride requests can outnumber available drivers on the road.

2. Prices Go Up:
To balance the demand and supply equation, prices may surge, ensuring that those in need of a ride can quickly connect with an available driver. This pricing strategy, known as surge pricing, is a dynamic system that keeps the Uber app a reliable choice even in high-demand scenarios.

3. Riders Choose:
When surge pricing is in effect, the Uber app notifies riders of the increased rates. Some riders may choose to pay the higher fare, while others might opt to wait a few minutes in the hope that the surge subsides.

How Surge Prices Are Calculated:
During surge pricing, you'll notice a multiplier to standard rates, an additional surge amount, or an upfront fare that includes the surge amount on your offer card. The surge pricing is city-specific, and Uber's service fee percentage remains consistent during these periods.

Because surge prices are updated in real time based on demand, they can change rapidly. Additionally, surge pricing is specific to different areas within a city, meaning that some neighborhoods may experience surge pricing while others do not.

Identifying Surge in the App:

To identify surge pricing in your city, watch for color changes on
the Uber map. When demand increases in a specific area, that
neighborhood will change color. Light orange areas indicate smaller
earning opportunities from surge, while dark red areas signify
larger potential earnings.

Tips for Navigating Surge Pricing:

1.   Stay Informed: Keep an eye on the app’s color-coded map
        to be aware of surge areas. This can help you strategically
        position yourself for maximum earning potential.
2.   Timing is Key: Understand the patterns of surge pricing
        in your city. Knowing when demand typically increases can
        help you capitalize on surge opportunities.
3.   Adapt and Adjust: Surge pricing is dynamic. Be prepared
        to adapt your strategy and adjust your location based on
        real-time changes in demand.
4.   Provide Excellent Service: Even during surge pricing,
        delivering excellent service is crucial. Satisfied
        passengers are more likely to accept and understand surge
        pricing.

Navigating surge pricing is both an art and a science. By
understanding the mechanics behind it and adopting a strategic
approach, you can turn surge moments into opportunities for
increased earnings on the rideshare highway.

ï¿½